Edmund Goldsmid, Herman Grube, Georg K. Kirchmayer, Martinus Schoock

Un-Natural History - Myths of ancient science - being a collection of curious tracts on the basilisk, unicorn, phoenix, behemoth or leviathan, dragon, giant spider, tarantula, chameleons, satyrs

Vol. 1

Edmund Goldsmid, Herman Grube, Georg K. Kirchmayer, Martinus Schoock

Un-Natural History - Myths of ancient science - being a collection of curious tracts on the basilisk, unicorn, phoenix, behemoth or leviathan, dragon, giant spider, tarantula, chameleons, satyrs

Vol. 1

ISBN/EAN: 9783337192730

Printed in Europe, USA, Canada, Australia, Japan

Cover: Foto ©Andreas Hilbeck / pixelio.de

More available books at **www.hansebooks.com**

[COLLECTANEA ADAMANTÆA.—XV.]

Un=Natural History,

OR

MYTHS

OF

ANCIENT SCIENCE;

Being a Collection of Curious Tracts on the Basilisk, Unicorn, Phœnix, Behemoth or Leviathan, Dragon, Giant Spider, Tarantula, Chameleons, Satyrs, Homines Caudati, &c.

NOW FIRST TRANSLATED FROM THE LATIN,

AND

Edited, with Notes and Illustrations,

BY

EDMUND GOLDSMID, F.R.H.S.,
F.S.A. (Scot.)

IN FOUR VOLUMES.

VOL. I.

PRIVATELY PRINTED.
EDINBURGH.
1886.

Introduction.

IT HAS seemed to me that the following tracts, on myths so strange, yet so widely credited in ancient times, could not fail to prove interesting, especially as the tracts themselves, written in the 17th century by German *savants*, and printed (very badly, by the way) at Wittemberg, Frankfort-on-Oder, &c., are quite unknown, not only in this country, but even in the land of their production. Of course, some few may have heard of Kirchmayer, but how many know even the names of Grübe or Schoochius?

The myths treated of in the following treatises are : the Basilisk, Unicorn, Phœnix, Behemoth, Dragon, Giant Spider, Tarantula, Chameleons, Satyrs, Tailed Men, and the Shining Lilies of Palestine.

George Caspard Kirchmayer, the author of the first six tracts, was born at Uffein-heim, in Franconia, in 1635. He became Professor at Wittemberg, and was a Fellow of the Royal Societies of London and Vienna. His principal works are : (1) Commentaries on Cornelius Nepos, Tacitus, and other classical authors; (2) Orations and various poems, of little value ; (3) De Corallo, Balsamo et Saccharo (1661, 4to); (4) De Tribulis (1692, 4to); (5) Pathologia Vetus et Nova ; (6) Philosophia Metallica ; (7) Institutiones Metallicæ; (8) The six Treatises here translated and printed, under the collective title of *Hexas disputationum Zoologicarum*, at Wittem-

Introduction. vii

berg, in 1661. This extremely rare volume, purchased by me at the Maidment sale, is a small 8vo. of some 180 pages. It is written in Latin, with numerous quotations in Greek, Hebrew, and Low German. Kirchmayer died in 1700.

Hermann Grübe was born at Lübeck, in 1633. He studied at Leyden, and became Professor of Medicine at Frankfort. He is said to have published several medical works, none of which are now ever read. His treatise, " De Ictu Tarantulæ," here translated, is, I believe, quite unknown to Bibliographers. It is a small 8vo tract of some 90 pages, published at Frankfort in 1679, and is bound up with my copy of Kirchmayer.

Martin Schoochius was born at Utrecht in 1614. After studying at that University he became successively Professor of Languages, of Eloquence and History, of

Physic, of Logic, and of Practical Philosophy at Utrecht, Deventer, Groningen, and lastly at Frankfort-on-Oder, where he died in 1669. He was a man of powerful energy and extensive knowledge, and took a delight in out-of-the-way researches; but by dint of trying to show erudition, he often lost sight of his subject which was swallowed up in long disgressions. He was, it appears, extremely satirical, and certainly managed to touch Vossius to the quick, for the latter calls him *Impudentissima Bestia* (In Append. Guidiana, p. 329). He wrote a prodigious amount of criticism, philosophy, history, general literature etc. Those works which are either known from the existence of copies in various libraries, or from allusions in the writings of others are: (1) *Exercitationes Variæ*, 1663, 4to, reprinted in 1688 under the title of *Martini Themidis Exercita-*

tiones; (2) A treatise on Butter; (3) On the aversion of some people for cheese; (4) On the egg and the chicken; (5) On inundations; (6) De Harengis, seu Halecibus, 8vo, 1667; (7) De Signaturis Fœtûs; (8) De Ciconiis; (9) De Scepticismo; (10) On sneezing; (11) De Cerevisia, 12mo, 1648; (12) De Turffis; (13) De Statu Reipublicæ Fœderati Belgii; (14) De Imperio Maritimo; (15) De Natura Soni; (16) De Nihilo; (17) De Lingua Helenistica; (18) An attack on Descartes entitled *Admiranda Methodus Novæ philosophiæ* and numerous religious tracts, of which all that can be said is, that they prove that Shoochius could write better about Butter, Satyres, Cheese, and Tailed Men than about matters of religion. The treatise which is here translated seems utterly unknown to all Bibliographers. It is a small 4to, abominably printed on atrocious paper, and bears the imprint of Frankfort-on-Oder, 1680. The only copy I know of is the one in my possession.

To me these learned and eccentric tracts have ever been extremely interesting. I trust they may prove so to my readers, and I have tried to increase their value by tracing out in the notes the various allusions of the text, and amplifying from such sources as I have had at my disposal, the subjects suggested rather than dwelt upon by these sage and quaint old writers of the 17th century.

EDMUND GOLDSMID.

EDINBURGH, 14*th March* 1886.

I.
On the Basilisk,

BY

GEORGE CASPARD KIRCHMAYER.

(1691.)

I.
On the Basilisk,

BY

GEORGE CASPARD KIRCHMAYER.

(1691.)

CHAPTER FIRST.

CONTENTS.

I. The frequent mention of the basilisk in sacred as well as in profane writings.
II. The etymology of the word. The kings of the brute creation ---their names.
III. A list of similar words with different meanings.
IV. Different names of the basilisk.

An Account of the Term "Basilisk."

I. The very frequent mention of the basilisk in sacred as well as profane writings demands some account of the word. This Isaiah, chap. xi. v. 8, has "The sucking child shall play on the hole of the asp, and the weaned child shall put his hand on the cockatrice' den." Megalotheander's Bible has, "He shall put his hand on the hole of the basilisk." In the same prophet, chap. xiv. 29, we read, "Out of the serpent's root shall come forth a cockatrice." Similarly, Luther's Bible has the words, "From the root of the serpent shall a basilisk come." Again, chap. lix. 5, "They hatch cockatrice' eggs." In Theander, again, we find, "They hatch basilisk's eggs." Compare Jeremiah, chap. viii. 17, and Proverbs, chap. xxiii. 32. The term basilisk was not unknown to the most ancient writers of heathendom, a fact which becomes clear from an inspection of the works of Pliny, Solinus, Lucan, Dioscoris, Galen, and others.

II. We have first of all to touch on the etymology of the word. The term basilisk arose in Greece, came into constant use in Latium, and remained among the Teutonic peoples. "Basilisk" is a diminutive from "basileus" (king), which is so termed from the king being the "basis" of the nation. We know, at least, that the king is the foundation of his people. This extremely poisonous serpent, therefore, gets its name of basilisk, or regulus, either from its virulence or through some fancied analogy from the diadem which it is said to carry on its head. The former derivation is probable from the fact that the basilisk is the most virulent of all the lesser kinds of reptiles, while it has, as a further characteristic, the extremely rapid action of its venom. For this reason it is thought to be shunned and feared by many of the animal creation. Among the greater kinds of reptiles we give the foremost place to the dragon, while we call the lordly eagle king of birds, the lusty lion, or rather, perhaps, the elephant, king of quadrupeds, and the dolphin prince among fishes. The fancied analogy between its crest and a crown, alluded to above, arises from three whitish excrescences, with which its head is so distinctly marked as to give the creature the appearance of carrying a cockscomb before it. John Eusebius says: "Its length is three hand's breadths, its body yellow, its head narrow and pointed, on which it has three excrescences, with whitish spots and in the shape of a crown, by reason of which it has been called the king of reptiles."*

III. We proceed to give a list of different meanings of the word. The term basilisk is hampered by many disadvantages arising from ambiguity. To such an extent is this the case, that we can neither place any reliance on the word itself nor on the thing denoted by it. In the first place, the term is applied to a little bird which we commonly call the trochilus, or golden-

* John Eusebius, a Jesuit, born at Nuremberg, and who became Professor of Physiology in the Academy of Madrid, is the author quoted. The passage occurs in the sixth book of his *Historia Natur.* folio 102.

crested wren. The trochilus or regulus (in Greek βασιλίσκος), is that timid bird which breeds in thorny copses, and is ornamented with a bunch of small reddish upright feathers on its head. It is half the size of the common sparrow, the harbinger, especially in May, of an unseasonable change of temperature, and is considered a cure for stone.

Secondly, the term is given to a certain kind of crowned or crested fish, which is called alaudæ or galeritæ by ornithologists. The first of zoologists, Ulysses Aldrovandus,* philosopher and doctor of Bologna, in his work on Fishes, bk. i. chap. 25, p. 42, has the following words: "Any one who wishes to refer the crowned or crested fishes, or any one of them, to the basilisks of Oppian, which he describes as living round the

---

* Was born at Bologna in 1525. He spent his life in researches in natural history, and, assisted though he was by several sovereigns, by the Senate of Bologna, and by his nephew, Cardinal Montalba, was reduced in his old age to comparative poverty. He died in 1605. His works fill 13 volumes folio, of which six only were actually written by him, the rest being composed by sundry learned men, according to his plan, by order of the Senate of Bologna. His works contain much that is superfluous, and show little method in arrangement. It is the dunghill of Ennius, and yet, in spite of all faults, natural history owes much to Aldrovandus.

rocky coast; he, in my opinion, would make no absurd mistake. Just as Rondeletius called his fish the galeritæ from its crest, and just as others have called the reptile which is marked by a white spot on its head, the basilisk, so also is a fish called the basilisk on account of a similar mark on its head."

Thirdly, the word is also applied, as Nurembergius* somewhere points out, to a kind of shrub. On this point botanists must be consulted.

Fourthly, as a proper name, the word basilisk belongs to a certain famous family in Spain, which gets the name of Basilisk or Blaskus, by reason of the bravery of its members, the meaning of the name being that, by a mere look, they can throw their enemies into confusion. The learned Nurembergius is our authority on this point.

IV. We subjoin a brief list of synonyms of the word. In Hebrew it is called Tzeph'a and Tziph'oni. These words are translated by Buxtorfius, in his lexicon, into regulus, basiliskus, and hœmorrhois, the most venomous of all the serpent tribe. In ancient Greek, it is called the basilisk, as we have mentioned above. In Latin it bears the names of regulus, gallo-bufo, crested asp, death-glancer, deadly reptile, &c.†

---

* This is John Eusebius, mentioned above, called thus from the place of his birth.

† For a description of the basilisk or cockatrice,

B

CHAPTER II.

ARGUMENT.

I. The basilisk is assigned a place in the (animal) creation.
II. Passages in Scaliger and Cardanus referred to.
III. A basilisk seen in Marcia. The existence to this day of monuments at Halle, in Saxony, at Basle and Zwicca, witnessing to basilisks having been seen. The basilisk most common in warmer countries.
IV. A basilisk seen at Warsaw, in Poland, by more than two thousand persons.
V. The story taken from D. Mosanus and John Pincierus.
VI. An enquiry into the opinion of Sperlingius.
VII. The same continued. Matthiolus noted. Sebizius praised.

On the Existence of the Basilisk.

I. To deny the existence of the basilisk is to carp at the evidence of men's eyes and their experiences in many different places. Accordingly, we allow the basilisk a place in nature, as the most deadly and venomous creature and plague in the animal creation.

---

taken from Topsell's " History of Serpents," published in 1658, see appendix. The Hebrew *Tzeph'a* was a monster more deadly than the *Pethen* (Gr. *aspis*, asp), which is variously translated in the authorised version of the Bible as *cockatrice* (Isaiah lix. 5), *adder* (Job xx. 14, and Proverbs xxiii. 32), and as *serpent* (Proverbs xxiii. 32, and Isaiah xi. 8). Shakespeare alludes to it at least twice; first in *Cymbeline*—

> " It is a *basilisk* unto mine eye
> Kills me to look on't."

We would have it understood we are not here maintaining that ridiculous and more than monstrous story of the manner of its birth, nor the deadly effect of its look, nor those other points which are more like old wives' stories than anything else. It is for the *existence* of this most venomous reptile that we are now contending.* Many, unless I am mistaken, will oppose us, but surely such men contradict the evidence of their own senses. To gainsay our senses and seek reasons for our position is surely nothing but folly and ignorance. We shall produce evidence not merely of a hearsay, but also of an ocular character ; the evidence of men who have seen the basilisk themselves.

And in Richard III :—
RICHARD—Thine eyes, sweet lady, have infected mine.
ANNE—Would they were *basilisk's*, to strike thee dead !
In his note on this passage, Mr Aldis Wright suggests that the name cockatrice is a corruption of crocodile.

* Of course we all know that *Basilisks* (a genus of Lizards) exist ; they belong to the Iguana family, and are confined to America. The basilisk of ancient times was " the King of Dragons and Serpents, whose breath withered up all vegetation, and whose very look was fatal to man." After this it is very disappointing to find that the Basilisk of modern naturalists, despite the formidable appearance of one variety, *Basiliscus mitratus*, is absolutely harmless !

II. Julius Cæsar Scaliger* in order to remove the suspicion of its being a myth, writes the following words :—" Since some have suspected that the stories told of the basilisk are fabulous, I shall write down what I have read in modern authors. When Leo was Pontifex Maximus, there was found lodged under the arch near the Temple of Lucia a basilisk, by the breath of which Rome was afflicted with a terrible plague, &c." Again, Hieronymus Cardanus † has the following passage :—" A certain pedlar had a serpent, which he had found in the ruins of a house that

---

* Born near Verona in 1484, he was first page to the Emperor Maximilian, then a successful soldier, and afterwards practised medicine in Guienne. He was a learned, honorable, charitable and truthful man, but conceited and wanting in good taste. The quotation above given is from his " *Exercitationes contra Cardanum*, No. 246, sect. 4. He died at Agen in 1558.

† Cardanus was an illegitimate child, born at Pavia in 1501. He was an extraordinary character; of a brilliant intellect, he was inconstant and obstinate, spiteful, extravagant and a lover of wine, women, and gaming. Having exhibited his wonderful knowledge and wild folly at Padua, Milan, Pavia and Bologna, he got himself locked up in the latter city; as soon as he was free, he went to Rome, obtained a pension from the pope, and starved himself to death in 1576, to accomplish his own prophecy that he would not live beyond the age of seventy-five. His principal works collected in 10 vols. folio, 1663) are : I. *De Subtilitate*

had been pulled down at Mediolanum.* Its head was the size of an egg, and very large in proportion to its body. I have preserved one of its bones. The teeth in each jaw are those of a viper. Its body is the size of a lizard, and of a similar shape, but it has only two feet, and its legs are too small for its size, which gives it a somewhat odd appearance."

III. Christopher Encelius, a man, in the opinion of Ulysses Aldrovandus, of the highest excellence in general culture, in his book on Metals (bk. iii. chap. 54) writes: "In the Marches † and in the jurisdiction of The Abbot of Zinnia, near the town of Luckenvald,‡ I had the good fortune to see such a serpent, which had been killed by a shepherd. The creature had a pointed head, was of a yellow and almost saffron colour, and had a length of three hand-breadths or more." Similarly, George Agricola § mentions that at Vienna,

---

(folio, 1550); II. *De rerum varietate*, (Basle, 1557. folio); III. His autobiography; etc., etc.

* Milan.

† Province of Brandenburg, Prussia.

‡ On the Nüthe, 30 miles south of Berlin.

§ Born at Glauchen in 1494. He acquired a wonderful knowledge of minerals and fossils, which was given to the world in a work *De re metallica*, Basle, 1561, folio, written in very elegant Latin. He died at Chemnitz in 1551. The allusion in the text is to a passage in a rare work of his, *De ortu et causis subterraneorum*, Basle, 1558, folio.

in Austria, there was once such a serpent, and that a picture of it could still be seen in the wall of a certain house. He says somewhat the same of the towns of Basle and Zwickau.* At Halle, in Saxony, there still stands a monument of unimpeachable authenticity, to commemorate the fact of a basilisk having been seen there. It is in warmer climates, especially where the most poisonous kinds of serpents find a home, that this deadly crested adder is most common. The Egyptians placed it among their hieroglyphics.† When they wished to indicate a man of evil tongue, they drew the picture of a basilisk. This gave rise to Lucan's verses: "Breathing forth its hisses, and striking out its poison, that contains every plague, the basilisk drives all the people far from its path, and reigns over the desolated sands."‡ Even the Ethiopians and Moors were far from being ignorant of the creature, for Lucan says: "What boots it, ye wretched Moors, to transfix the basilisk with

---

* A small town in Bohemia, at the foot of the Lausitz Gebirge. There is another town of the name in Saxony, on the Mulde.

† This passage would support Mr. Aldis Wrights' contention, mentioned in the note on page 19.

‡ *Sibilaque effundens cunctasque tenentia pestes,*
Ante venena necens, latè sibi submovet omne
Vulgus, et in vacua regnat Basiliscus arena.

your spear? Swift up the blade the poison speeds, and invades the hand."*

IV. But evidence more trustworthy and quite beyond cavil is forthcoming. At Warsaw, in Poland, in the sight of more than two thousand persons, a basilisk was seen, which had been taken from the rubbish of a fallen house, by means of an iron rake. D. Mosanus, Cassellanus, and John Pincier (Guesses, bk. iii. 23) have given a full account of this most remarkable event in all its details. The account, however, of each of these writers is extremely prolix; accordingly, not to weary the reader with a too full account, and in order not to appear to heap up a mere empty crop of words, it is our intention to adduce, with a strict regard for truth, only such particular points as bear on the present subject.

V. "In the year 1587, there lived at Warsaw, in Poland, a certain man named Machæropaeus. To pass the time, a child of this man, together with the little girl of a neighbour, as is the way with children of the tender age of five years, thought of an amusing game. They determined to enter the underground cellar of a house which had fallen into ruins 30 years before. As soon as they entered it, however, they fell to the lowest

---

* *Quid prodest miseri, Basiliscus cuspide, mauri, Transactus? Velox currit per tela venenum, Invaditque manum.*

steps, and expired. When the dinner-hour came round, their respective mothers asked if any one knew where their children were. No information could be got. The wife of Machæropaeus sent her maid to call in the children. She went out, and spied the children lying on the lowest steps of the cellar. Thinking they were overcome with sleep, she called again and again, and shouted to waken them. Her shouts, which had almost made her hoarse, produced no effect. What could be the matter? The woman took courage, and went down the steps to waken the children who were sleeping too deeply for any shaking to wake them. And, lo! at once (as was noticed) she herself sank down beside the children, and breathed her last. The mistress, who had seen her servant enter, ran to the place in astonishment, and out of her senses, not knowing what she ought to do, stood stupefied. A rumour at once got abroad, the citizens ran together, they were in a state of doubt, and deliberated what was to be done. The affair, meanwhile, was brought before the Consul and Senate. They gave orders to have the bodies drawn out with fire-hooks.* When this had been done they were found to be swollen like drums, their tongues had swelled, and the colour

---

* Long poles with iron hooks at the end, which were used by firemen on the continent in the 17th century.

of their skins was dark, while their eyes protruded from their sockets, as large as half an hen's egg. At the request of the Consul, the Chamberlain and an old man, physician to the King, called Benedictus, came to see the tragic spectacle. The latter's conjecture was, that a serpent of most deadly kind was living in the deserted cellar, and that the air in it was poisoned by its deadly breath, which was prevented from escaping. Seeing, moreover, that the weak nature of man could not stand against it, he concluded that it was a basilisk which had its den in the cellar.

On being asked by what means the truth of the affair could be found out, he replied that some one should be sent into the cellar, furnished with a covering of mirrors, facing in all directions. For, said he, the basilisk will at once die if it sees its own image. There were there, at that time, two men lying under sentence of death, which were to be executed within three days, one a Pole, the other a Silesian. The name of the Silesian was John Faurer. An offer was made to these men, to see if one would descend into the cellar, and hunt for the serpent, on condition of obtaining a pardon. The Silesian at once embraced the offer. Accordingly, his whole body was covered with leather, his eyelids fastened down on the pupils, one hand was armed with an iron rake, and the other with a blazing torch. In the presence of MORE THAN

TWO THOUSAND PERSONS, who looked on in the highest excitement, the man descended into the cellar, a mass of mirrors from head to foot. After an hour's examination of every chink and corner of the cellar, without any trace of the serpent being found, he asked for a fresh torch to be thrown down to him. On being asked his reason for this request, he said that there was another cellar next to the one he was in, but approach to it was barred by rubbish. Whilst endeavouring to penetrate this, he happened to move his eyes to the left, and suddenly spied the long looked for serpent, lying in a niche of the wall. On signifying the fact by shouting to those who were crowded round the entrance, the chief physician bade him take the brute up with the iron rake, and carry it out of the darkness of the cellar into the broad daylight. This was done and seen by all. The Chief Physician, as soon as he saw the creature, pronounced it a basilisk. It was the size of an ordinary fowl. In its head it had somewhat the appearance of an Indian cock. Its crest was like a crown, partly covered with a bluish colour. Its back was covered with several excrescent spots, and its eyes were those of the toad. It was covered all over with the hues of venomous animals, which gave it a general tawny tinge. Its tail was curved back, and bent over its body, of a yellowish hue beneath, and of the same colour as the toad at its extremity." This description, though somewhat diffuse, is perhaps, gentle reader, not unwelcome.

VI. From this story some estimate of this most venomous creature may be formed. That incomparable student of Nature, Sperling,* had too great an insight into the subject to attempt to deny absolutely the existence of the basilisk. But while he observed that by this creature was to be understood a poisonous asp, he at least had the sense to refute those old wives' stories which are connected with the subject, and which will be found refuted in our subsequent investigations. Thus, in his public lectures on Zoology (Bk. vi., chap. iii., sect. 2), in speaking of the asp, he comes to the following conclusion :—" If there is such a thing as the basilisk, it is an asp. Now, the poison of this creature is most deadly, especially in warm climates. It is man's nature to exaggerate everything, and to make two or three false additions to every simple fact."

VII. Again our beloved Professor, in the year 1637, in which he first became known to the world, and in the fortieth public discussion which he held on the mysteries of nature, wished the following question to be propounded :—"*Is the basilisk* or cockatrice able to kill men by looking

* Born at Zeuchfeld, in Thuringia, in 1603; became Professor of Physics at Wittemberg, where he died in 1658.

at them?" The answer was made on the authority of Pliny (Bk. 8, cap. 21) and Ælian (Book vii., cap. 2), to the effect that there is a spring among the western tribes of Africa, called the Niger, and considered by some to be the source of the Nile, where these creatures are found, and that they are capable of causing death by being looked on, by reason of the bright rays of light which they emit. Bodinus gives an opinion nearer the truth in his third book of his *Theatrum Naturale*, when speaking of the breeding of serpents; and Neander[*] is right in approving it in the following words:—"I cannot think that an animal should have been created by the Great Artificer, of such a deadly kind as to cause the death of the rest of the animal creation merely by looking at them. But we are safe in believing that the basilisk, the most deadly of all reptiles, causes death by its breath, which is of the most noxious and pestilential nature. This poisonous breath is of the most subtle kind, and may be inhaled into the body, and as soon as it penetrates the system, it rushes to the vitals and destroys the spirit of life, etc."

[*] John Neander must not be confounded with either of the two Michael Neanders. John was the author of *Tobacologia*, a curious and very scarce work on Tobacco and its uses. It is a 4to volume, published at Leyden in 1622. The allusion in the text is to a passage in his *Syntagma* (folio, 1623). He was a doctor at Bremen. Nothing else is known of him.

We cannot but wonder what grounds Mathiolus* has (Comment., Bk. vi., last chapter) for giving credence to the fabulous tales that have been handed down by tradition concerning this creature. Although Mathiolus has adduced three petty reasons in support of his position, yet he has been satisfactorily answered by Melchior Sebizius,† a most learned man, in his Appendix to his Treatise on Medicine, applied to the case of diseases among young men. There, among other things, he brings forward the evidence of Hieronymus Mercurialis‡

* Peter Andrew Matthiolus, a celebrated doctor and elegant litterateur, was born at Sienna about 1500. His *Commentaries on Dioscoris* (Venice, 1548, 4to) and other works show much research but considerable credulity. He died of the plague in 1577.

† Sebizius, born 1578, died 1674, canon of Strasburg, was created Count Palatine by Ferdinand II. His principal works are :—I. Commentaries on Galen ; II. Exercitationes Medicæ ; III. Miscellaneæ questiones medicæ ; IV. Speculum medicinæ practicum (2 vols. 8vo, 1661.)

‡ Born at Forli, (ancient Forum Lirii), in the province of that name on the Adriatic, in 1530, died there in 1596. He was celebrated for his knowledge of Medecine. Unlike most men of talent, he left behind him a huge fortune for those days, 120,000 crowns. He was a good aud a wise man. His principal works are :—I. De arte gymnastica, Venice, 1587, 4to, a curious book on the gymnastics of the ancients ; II. De Morbis Mulierum, 4to, 1601 ; III. De Morbis Puerorum, 4to, 1584 ; IV. Medecina practica, folio, 1627.

Bk. i., chap. 21, on Poisons and Poisonous Diseases), who declares that, at the Court of the Emperor Maximilian, he saw the body of a basilisk, which was preserved among the treasures of the Palace. Having proved now that we must assign a place in creation to the basilisk, we have still to investigate its character. We shall deal briefly with the matter, in order to pass on to the discussion of other subjects. Let us set to work.

CHAPTER III.

CONTENTS.

I. A description of the basilisk.
II. Falsehood of the statement that the basilisk springs from the egg of an old cock.
III. Reasons adduced.
IV. The empty contradiction of L. Lemnius on this point.
V. The position of Eucebius and Ferrantes Imperatus. We must not believe everything we hear from any quarter without consideration and reason. The source of error.
VI. The false and fabulous story of men being killed by the mere gaze of the basilisk. This not even true of the wolf.
VII. Natural antipathy between the basilisk and the weasel and cock.

The Nature and Properties of the Basilisk.

I. The basilisk is a crested asp, the most deadly of its kind, and the greatest enemy of man. It is marked by many white excrescences, has a somewhat large head, and is full of most virulent poison. By means of this (*i.e.*, by exhalation and by vitiating the circumambient air) it impregnates the surrounding space with its deadly property. This poison, by an obscure antipathy which it bears to all created things, at once chokes and suffocates anything warmblooded. The above is not a definition, but somewhat of a description, containing more than is essential to a definition. It is an asp, as we said, by reason of its deadly, virulent, and cunning nature, though it has not the same length of body as the rest of the asp tribe. We do not believe the basilisk is a common reptile, nor, except in the deserts of warmer climates, is it largely found.

Again, we have called it "crested" not literally, as we speak of the barnyard cock, but analogically. It has, as may be seen by a comparison of authors, something analogous to a crown or crest. Hence it gets the name of regulus or basilisk. It is called a "most deadly" asp from the effect of its poison, seeing that the injury it inflicts with its terrible venom is the most deadly of all. Every serpent is an enemy of man and every living creature, but this creature takes the palm for deadliness.

The punishment of mankind, in retribution for the crime committed against the great Creator, is that the very serpents should be armed against us.

Had our first parents remained in the state in which they were originally created, the power of subduing these creatures in common with the rest of creation would have remained in their hands without injury or danger. So terrible is the significance to man of a sin against his Creator. Such is the terrible bane which serpents are to us now; for it was disguised in their form that that preternatural old Dragon, the slanderer of God and man, originally made his assault upon mankind. We need not give an explanation of the other words which were used in our description of the basilisk. It is a matter of mere experience, and will become clear from the subsequent remarks. In order, however, to enable us to distinguish with safety between true metal and dross, between false and true, we must remove from our conception of this creature those traditions, whether they go under the name of dreams or serious facts, which have been handed down to us on the subject.

II. The story, which is commonly credited, of the basilisk springing from the egg of a decrepit cock, nine years old, and being hatched by a toad, is utterly false, and without foundation. We shall give the story which men of little brains tell us. They say the basilisk is born from a cock. The cock, they say, when decrepit, brings forth an egg, from which the basilisk springs. Many things, however, must conduce to this end. The egg must be placed in a warm heap of dung, which hatches the creature; another version is that the hatching is done by a repulsive toad. Then a chicken is hatched, which has a tail like a snake, but the rest of its body is that of a cock. Those who say they have witnessed the production of this creature, declare that the egg has no shell, but a skin of such extreme strength, that it can withstand the severest blows, &c. We know this much, that if this is the case, there never has been, is, or will be, anywhere, such a creature as the basilisk. Who is so bereft of reason as to allow himself to be persuaded That a real egg can come from a common cock? *Real*, I mean, for it cannot be denied that in some cocks there is found a small globule of whiteish excrement formed by putrefaction. "For it is quite possible" (I use the words of John Eusebius, of Nuremberg, Royal Physician at Madrid, in Spain) "that when cocks have passed the time of life when they are able to perform their functions, the excrement inclosed within their bodies is coagulated into an egg by a process of putrid concoction," &c. (Hist. Nat., lib. 6, fo. 102.) The learned Peter Lauremberg says:—"There does indeed exist in the body of the cock a growth with a white skin, but without a shell. But the cock does not produce this as the hen its egg, nor can anything living come out of it. The hen lays eggs, not the cock."

III. Who, in fact, can easily believe that a cock, the most wholesome of animals, can possibly produce a creature of the most loathsome and hideous kind? Who can listen for one moment to this nonsensical and most monstrous story of birth? A serpent comes from a serpent, a cock from a hen, but a basilisk from a cock, never! Can any one believe that a cock when grown old, and with its powers destroyed, when almost no further strength is left it, can possibly conceive and produce an egg? What is this hideous toad that can possibly come to the spot, led by the scent, and in the regular order of nature sit on the egg at the right moment to hatch it? Whoever you are that can tell such a barefaced falsehood without blushing, tell us, in sooth, have you ever seen such things? Have you watched them carefully? Have you studied them? No, no. Let this cock's egg, which you have hauled in head and ears, crumble into lime or dung.

IV. Lævinus Lemnius,* a most excellent doctor, tells us, however, that he maintains it as a fact, proved from his own experience, that the cock not only produces an egg, but itself sits on it. He says:—In the State of Ziriczee, and in the

---

* Born at Ziriczee in Zeeland in 1505; he was the author of I. "*De occultis naturæ miraculis* 8vo; II. *De astrologia*, 8vo; III. *De plantis biblicis*, 12mo, 1591.—He died in 1568.

limits of this island, there are two old cocks which not only sat on their own eggs, but were with difficulty driven with sticks from the work of hatching them." And he adds that the people of the place, having conccived the idea that the basilisk comes from such an egg, smashed the eggs and strangled the cock. The answer of Ulysses Aldrovandus to these words is, as usual, most judicious. "What this writer and others affirm I could never be persuaded to believe by any number of oaths. I am so far from being able to believe either that a cock should place its egg amongst dung to let it be fecundated by its heat, or that a basilisk is generated by toads who hatch it, that I would rather consider the whole thing a joke. At the same time, I do not deny that the cock secretes within itself, especially at the end of its life, when no longer able to perform its function, something like an egg, which is produced by a process of putrefaction. But that it brings forth an egg, complete and furnished with a shell, I cannot possibly believe. Reason tells us this can only be done in the womb. Just as no one thinks of maintaining that a complete fœtus can be produced by a man, so neither can one come from a cock."

V. The boasting, therefore, of Lævinus and Christopher Encelius, no less than of the Neapolitan physician, Ferrans Imperatus, whom they mention, is useless. They said they had not only seen, but had in their possession, such eggs, which had been laid by cocks. Surely not every one who makes a boast of the wonders of nature is to be trusted. Besides, they who believe in anything easily are easily deceived also. We must take Nature into our confidence. Her powers must be explored; their nature, effcacy, and antipathies will become clear after an intimate inquiry. I suspect the fable of Hermes gave rise to this falsehood. Hermes had said that the regulus was produced from the egg of the cock in the womb or in dung. This, however, he did not intend to be understood about the true basilisk, but about the elixir which changes metals. We may compare Eusebius (Hist. Nat., Bk. iv., chap. 29, fo. 120).

VI. But it is a false and groundless statement, that the basilisk is able by a mere look to kill either a man or any other animal which it is the first to see. Galenus, in his book on the action of antidotes, says:—" The basilisk is a yellowish creature, furnished with a threefold crown on its forehead, and is of such a nature that merely by being seen or heard when hissing it kills those who see or hear it. And any animal whatsoever touching it, even when dead, dies immediately."

The fictions which Pliny, who in his writings is more celebrated for style than for accuracy of statement (Nat. Hist. Bk. 8, cap. 21), and Ælian tell us of, are of the same nature. Much confusion and obscurity accordingly reign in regard to the strength and poison of the regulus, as Pliny calls it. The remark of Bodinus* is a good one. He says, "Who has ever seen it, if it kills by merely being seen?" As if, forsooth, vision took place by emission of rays, and not rather by the reception of sensible particles. The great Scaliger asks for nothing but stripes for such collectors of falsehoods. The vulgar have some stories like these about the wolf, which Cardanus was neither tired nor ashamed of defending. This was the reason of the severe criticism he received at the hands of Schaliger. "Be wise in time," he says, "and let this be a mark of my affection for you. I want to hear none of these many silly

---

*Jean Bodin, born at Anger in 1530, was a favorite of Henry III. In 1589, he followed the Duke of Alençon to England, where his great work, *De Republicâ*, became a text book at Cambridge. One of his most curious works is *La Démonomanie, ou Traité des Sorciers*, Paris, 1587, 4to, wherein he maintains that he had a familiar spirit that used to touch him on the right ear when he did a good action, and on the left when he did a bad one. Having convinced himself that one could not catch the plague at 60 years of age, he took no precautions, and died of that disease in 1596. The quotation is from his *Theatrum Naturæ*, bk. 3, p. 306. (1596, 8vo). This book was suppressed, and is consequently rare.

stories you have included in your books." He continues, "But let us treat of the subject of sympathy, which you have touched on both coldly and in a childish manner. In this respect you require some help. For what is its nature? Why do men grow dumb when they see a wolf? Because there is a power in its eyes, you say. But is there any if I do not see its eyes? Its eyes do not penetrate a man's back, do they? or pass through his head to his tongue? I should like these assertors of falsehood to be beaten with as many rods as the times I have been seen by a wolf without any harm to my voice. I know for certain I have been seen no less than three times by a wolf when hunting. Once by one which was crouching in the middle of a thicket, again by one on the brow of a mountain. The third occasion was when one had carried off a little child, and the wolf, while hidden in a crop of hemp, fully grown, every now and then raised its head to get a view of the hunters. One of the poor child's companions exclaimed: "Oh, what a large dog!" My companions and myself were seen by the beast, while none of us saw it. We were so far from being struck dumb, that by shouting at the top of our voices we first of all scared it away, and then, following it up, secured its victim, though unfortunately no longer in life." Let a similar test be made in the case of the basilisk, that death-glancer, forsooth! It will be an easy thing to show what constitutes an act of vision. When looking on an object no particles of matter are made to vibrate from our eyes, but, on the contrary, we receive the images of objects which are represented in the crystalline lens. The chief authority to consult is Athanasius Kircher* on the Magnetic Art (Bk. iii., part 9, chap. 1, p. 777).

VII. If the story is really true, it is a singular fact that the basilisk flees from the presence of a weasel or cock. Men are to be found who, if

---

* Kircher was a Jesuit of Fulda, in Hesse Cassel. He was a good Mathematician and a very learned man, and was Professor at Witzburg, in Franconia till driven out by the Swedish armies. He retired to France, and ultimately to Rome, where he died in 1680, at the age of 70. His writings were extremely numerous, some being very curious and others very rare. To the former class belong the book mentioned in the text, *Prolusiones magneticæ*, Rome, 1654, folio; Arca Noë, folio; Turus Babel, folio, Amsterdam 1679. To the latter, *Ædipus Ægyptiacus*, Rome, 1652-3, 4 vols. folio, on Hieroglyphics. He was an enthusiastic antiquarian, and some good stories are related of him. One might be taken as the original of the famous stone story in Pickwick. Some young men, knowing his weakness, engraved a number of meaningless signs on a stone and buried it where they knew Kircher was about to build. It was of course found and carried to Kircher, who, after many days and nights of labour, produced a most interesting reading of the unknown symbols!

they enter a room in which there is a cat, though the latter be shut up in a basket, will yet begin to tremble, perspire profusely, and sometimes faint. In the same way cattle, on coming to a place at which two or three days previously one of their kind was slaughtered, begin to bellow, and are seized with fright. So mysterious is Mother Nature! Thus do the greatest curiosities lie hid in the smallest facts. On the subject of the deadly enmity between the cock and the basilisk, Ulysses Aldrovandus quotes a passage from Solinus.* "It is said that this creature (wonderful to relate), should it happen to see a cock, begins to tremble, and on hearing it approaching, is struck with such terror as to die on the spot. Travellers through the vast tracts of Cyrenia, which are infested with this singular pest, recognising this fact, take with them as a companion a cock. The object of carrying this cock is to drive away this deadly reptile by its crowing."

Thus there is no evil so great or serious as not to have some antidote to it. Death alone would be invincible, did not the mind despise it and look forward with eagerness to hopes of future

---

* Solinus, a writer of the end of the first century. He has been surnamed "Pliny's Monkey," as he apes the style of the master. Aldrovandus quotes him, as stated in the text, in the 14th book of his *Ornithologia*, fol. 115.

joy, and thus triumph even over the greatest hardships destiny has in store. Of the weasel, John Eusebius, of Nuremberg, gives a definition in the following terms:—" The wisdom of Providence, in order to avoid leaving a pest of this nature without a deadly enemy, created the weasel, which is as powerful a foe to the basilisk as the latter is to man." So much for the basilisk, that most extraordinary of all creatures.

Ten Additional Zoological Dicta.

I. The serpent by and in itself cannot possibly understand the incantation of poisoners, whether male or female, did not that old dragon, the betrayer of the world, the slanderer of mankind, the Devil, lurk disguised under the outward form of a serpent, and play off his wonderful tricks of deceit and imposture on those less cunning than himself.

II. The tales told about that unique bird, the Phœnix, if accepted literally, are quite fabulous; if otherwise, they become mere parables. Wonder should never lead to credulity, as is so truly pointed out by Julius Cæsar Scaliger in his 233rd exercitation.

III. We shall deal very shortly with the question as to whether the Griffin should have a place in the animal creation, a question which is raised by B. Franzius* (Hist. Animalium, c. 38), who says this winged quadruped is of such strength and courage, that it can overcome eight lions and one hundred eagles, and carry an armed man up into the air. The words of Gabriel Rollenhagen† are enough. He says, "When the Saxon and Scythian armies entered Greece, and had landed on the coast panting for spoil, they used to plunder, beyond the walls of the towns, where they could not be rescued, men of the country, who fled before them. These they pursued and followed on horseback as fast as they could, shouting '𝕲𝖗𝖊𝖎𝖋, 𝖌𝖗𝖊𝖎𝖋 𝖉𝖊𝖓 𝕶𝖊𝖗𝖑!' The term, accordingly, does not owe its origin to the form of any living creature, but to a poetic expression, and does not apply to a product of nature, but to a product of song."

IV. The opinion of those who believe the whole race of unicorns to have perished in the flood is ridiculous.‡

---

* This is an error: the Christian name of Franzius being Wolfgang. He was a Lutheran theologian, born in 1564 at Plaven, in Voigtland, and Professor at Wittemberg, where he died in 1620. The work alluded to is his "*Animalium Historia sacra*," 12mo., 1665, a curious but rare book.

† I cannot find the quotation. The only work of Rollenhagen I can trace, besides a few plays, is his *Froschmunster*, an epic in the style of Homer's *Batrachomyomachia*. Rollenhagen died in 1609, aged 57.

‡ This statement is the text of our next tract.

V. We have come to the conclusion that the song attributed to the swan (when dying) is a pure figment. Many reasons induce us to take this view, and we have the support of Scaliger and that most learned man Sperlingius.

VI. Although the renewal of moulted feathers is one thing, and the renewal of vigorous youth quite another, yet Judeus Appella believes that eagles renew their youth. (In support of this fable, consult R. Dav. Kimchi,* *ex* R. Subadia, super. chap. 40, Esai.) †

VII. It would be the part of a very weak man to believe that brute beasts can naturally converse among themselves. Melampus‡ and Hieronymus

---

* Rabbi David Kimchi, a Spaniard, one of the most learned Hebrew scholars of the 13th century, was the selected arbitrator between the synagogues of Spain and France in the dispute about the books of Maimonides. His principal works are *Michlol* (that is, *Perfection*), a Hebrew Grammar, printed at Venice in 1541, 8vo; *Dictionarium Talmudicum*, Venice, 1506, folio, and a work on Hebrew roots, 1555, 8vo.

† The most curious book, on the question of the possible renewal of youth, I have met with, is "Hermippus Redivivus," which I have reprinted in this present series.

‡ A famous sage of ancient times, said to have lived about 1380 B.C. Many works were printed from the 15th to the 17th centuries as his. One of these is probably here alluded to.

Fabricius,* of Aquapendente, among modern writers have opposed this theory. (See the latter's "Treatise on the language of animals.)

VIII. Man alone can, properly speaking, laugh, weep, or talk in a natural manner. Neither ape, crocodile, magpie or nightingale can do so in the same way.

IX. To assign a place in the animal creation to what are called the Ephemeridæ, which are born in the morning and die at night, is such an absurd doctrine that we dismiss it without further words.†

X. To believe that the Pelican, a bird with a curved beak, tears its own breast, and restores its young to life by bleeding itself, is to dream.

---

* Jerome Fabricius, better known as Aquapendente (the place of his birth), was the pupil and successor of Fallopius in the Chair of Anatomy at Padua. His anatomical works were printed at Leyden in 1738, folio, and his surgical writings were collected and published in 1723, folio. He laboured more for glory than interest, and his friends having made him various presents as a reward for his disinterestedness, he placed them in a cabinet with the inscription :

" Lucri neglecti lucrum."

He died in 1603.

† In spite of Kirchmayer, we know that the Ephemeridæ, of which our English genus is the may-fly, only exist a few hours when they have reached this final stage of life.

II.

On the Unicorn,

BY
GEORGE CASPARD KIRCHMAYER.

PREFACE.

AMONG the pleasant sights of Paradise, the picture of the animal creation, both small and great, obeying the nod of primeval man, is by no means the least pleasing. There one might see lordly lions, huge and strong elephants, Rhinoceroses and Monoceroses, at the word of command, making their appearance, and allowing the yoke to be placed on them by the hand of man. Again, one might see other animals with faculties innumerable, and beauty unspeakable, coming at the command of the glorious Creator, and receiving the names corresponding to their natures. This was the first meeting of the animal creation. The second was a mournful one indeed; but even it was wonderful in the extreme. For when Divine Justice changed to severe anger, on account of the grievous crimes of men, and determined to destroy the wicked from the face of the earth by a flood of avenging waters, which was to sweep away the guilt of mankind, at the instigation of the Most High many pairs of animals were collected (of fishes there was no need), and received into the ark, which had lately been built, until it was quite full.

What were your thoughts, Noah, when you acted as host to the crowds of the whole animal creation? or when the stench from the interior oppressed your senses, and, without, the heaps of dead men and animals floated about, and the huge waves threatened you with instant death. You did not, methinks, revile your God, but repeated your prayers night and day. With Him as your stay, not only could you be free from anxiety, but safe in the fullest sense of the word. God consoled you, He helped you, He was the constant guardian of you and yours. Tell us, is it not wrong to think that a single species perished and became extinct then, when such a great God took in hand the charge of all. But just as there is no kind of creature so beautiful as not to perform the filthy functions of nature, so there is nothing so sacred as to escape the violation of the audacious. Over the whole world it is a common saying that the unicorn perished and became extinct at the flood, and that not a single individual of the Monoceros species survived. We shall correct this injustice, and shall, with God's help, find a means of putting a stop to this universal blasphemy.

On the Unicorn.

CHAPTER I.

ARGUMENT.

1. Nature and formation of the term Monoceros.
2. A part of Christ's Cross is called "Unicorn."
3. The term applied to a mineral.
4. Explanation of analogous uses of the word continued.
5. The existence of unicorn fish.
6. Unicorn birds seen by the Lusitanians.
7. The one-horned vipers used by Cleopatra. Cardanus censured.
8. Single-horned beetles seen by Bartholinus between Salerno and Naples.
9. The one-horned ass of India.
10. A one-horned horse presented to the late John George I., Elector of Hanover. Similar creatures seen frequently by other persons.
11. Single-horned oxen and cows found. To this head the wild oxen of Russia are to be referred.
12. An account of the wonderful animal called the oryx.
13. The rhinoceros, the deadly enemy of the elephant.
14. The rhinoceros not to be confounded with the monoceros. Cardanus blamed and defended. Scaliger praised.
15. An inquiry into the term unicorn, both as a substantive and as a creature. Various synonyms of the term.

I. The term monoceros is originally of Greek origin, and comes from *monos*, meaning one, and *keras*, meaning a horn. In the Attic method of pronunciation the word is accented on the antepenultimate syllable. Among the Latins the term unicorn (*i.e.*, furnished with only one horn) has exactly the same meaning. By some writers, such as Bartholomew, of England, Nicolas Perotta, and Eusebius, of Nuremberg, the word *unicornuus* is used instead. Nestor, of Novarre, under the word *unicorn*, page 102, says that it can also be declined as *unicornium*. John of Japua speaks in almost the same terms, when he proves that *mon cerus* and *monoceri* are possible terms. Such matters are, however, to be left to philological scholars to decide. It is our duty to explain with care and accuracy the common signification of the word. Our exertions in this respect must be conducted with greater perseverance when we consider what a great advantage it is to have truth cleared of the labyrinths of falsehood. It is my opinion, indeed, that the majority of the false stories about the monoceros, which are not only monstrous but obscure, could not have arisen except through an indistinct apprehension of what the term signifies.

II. The term unicorn is one in universal use, not only in matters of art but in those of nature. That it belongs and is applied to the first of these two classes is clearly seen by the evidence of Irenæus, Justinus, and Tertullian, according to whom the middle part of the main beam of Christ's Cross was called "the unicorn." A

passage in Deuteronomy, chap. xxiii. 17,* afforded Tertullian an opportunity of making this statement. The following are the words he uses in chap. xi. of the book written against the Jews:—
"Christ," he says, "was therein meant to be represented by the bull, by reason of his double attitude towards men—his attitude of severity to some as their judge, his attitude of clemency to others as their Saviour. The horns of this bull were the extreme points of the cross-beam, while the 'unicorn' was the middle plank of the main beam." These words of Tertullian have not, however, been able to withstand the close scrutiny of criticism.† Not only D. Georgius Calixtus, in his notice of the Cross, written at Leipsic, but Dn. Dibberrus, in his account of the Crucifixion, have given the meaning of the word. The Cross was called unicorn partly because it had a sharp curved point, partly because it was placed in the middle of the beam, as the horn is in the forehead of the animal, and had no other part of the structure to correspond to it. (See Magnus, son of

---

* "His glory is like the firstling of his bullock, and his horns are like the horns of unicorns, with them he shall push the people together to the ends of the earth : and they are the ten thousands of Ephraim, and they are the thousands of Manasseh."

† Balzac used to say that the obscurity of Tertullian's style was like the blackness of Ebony, very brilliant.

Bartholinus Magnus, On the Unicorn, chap. 23, page 149, and following.)

III. The term is applied to natural products, both "mineral" and "natural." For instance, in Bohemia, Thuringia, Moravia, and in certain districts of Misnia, stones are dug from some of the mines, which possess a powerful virtue against Epilepsy, against malignant fevers and other diseases of less note.

Sennertus,* the great doctor of Germany, is worth quoting on this point. He says, "Among porous stones, that species deserves notice which is commonly said to be the unicorn's horn. Others call it a fossil-horn. In Thuringia, Bohemia, and other places, such horns are found, and not only horns but other bones which have the name of being good for healing wounds and broken bones, and for curing sores." Especially are the following words to be considered: "These horns, experience has taught us, possess great power, especially in curing Epilepsy, malignant fevers, plague, bowel

---

* Daniel Sennert, or Sennertus, was the son of a shoemaker of Breslaw. He was born in 1572, became Professor of Medecine at Wittemburg, and died of the plague in 1637. His works, in 3 vols., folio, Venice 1640, or in 6 vols., folio, Lyons, 1676, are a complete compendium of Medical Science up to his day, and are far more valuable than many highly-raised modern productions.

complaints in children, and other diseases. From this circumstance they are commonly sold as unicorn's horn." The story that the whole race of unicorns perished at the Flood derives plausibility from the fact that, at the present day, horns, which were covered over with the sediment left by the waters of the Flood, and which have lain all this time buried in the earth, are in many places dug up again. With this remark, however, we will deal later on.

IV. At the present point we have to give a clear and systematic account of the different cases in which the term Monoceros is applied to animals. We cannot gain the desired haven of truth until we pass over the distortions and ambiguities that intercept our path.

Creatures that swim, that fly, that creep, that wade, besides insects, all claim the name unicorn. As far as the first of these divisions is concerned, the claim seems just, as certain Batavians, on returning from the East Indies, in 1601, brought with them a huge sea-beast, which had a large single horn. The great Clusius has left us a picture of it. (Bk. ii.)* The existence of a kind of

---

* The Narwhal (Monodon Monoceros), or Sea Unicorn is evidently meant. In the male, one tooth, usually the left, is developed into a long, straight-pointed tusk or "horn" of solid ivory, the surface being marked with spiral ridges or grooves. This

creature called the Hippopotamus is affirmed by some, but doubted by others. Whatever the truth may be, it is a fact that in the year 1576 Martin Frobisher * came across a fish-unicorn among the huge ice-fields, which had a horn that protruded about two cubits in front of its nose. (*History of East India*, Book ii. chap. 26.) Olaus Magnus,† Bk. xxi. chap. 10, on the Monoceros, says: "The

---

enormous tusk varies from six to eight feet in length. Occasionally both teeth are developed into tusks. The Narwhal varies from ten to sixteen feet in length, and the tusk is generally more than half the length of the body. It has been conjectured that the horn is employed in spearing fish, or in stirring up food from the bottom; but this would place the females at a great disadvantage. As the tusks are frequently found broken, they may be weapons used for fighting, developed like the horns of ungulates through sexual selection.

*Martin Frobisher was of a Devonshire family. In 1575 he sailed on his first voyage of discovery, and reached the latitude of 63°. In 1577, he undertook a second voyage, but returned without accomplishing his object. He subsequently greatly distinguished himself against the Armada. In 1594, he landed in Brittany, to besiege the fort of Cordon, near Brest, but was wounded, and died of his wounds at Plymouth.

† Olaus Magnus was Archbishop of Upsala, in succession to his brother. His great work, *Historia Gentium Septentrionalium*, Rome, 1555, folio, contains much that is curious, but the author was undoubtedly very credulous. Olaus died at Rome about 1560.

Monoceros is a sea-monster" (I would have preferred if Olaus had abstained from the use of this word, which casts a slur on Nature) "which has on its forehead a very large horn, by means of which it can pierce and wreck vessels with which it comes in contact, and destroy a large number of persons who may be on board. But in this case, the love of a Divine Providence gives a source of escape to the seaman, for in spite of its ferocity, it has such an extreme slowness of motion, that, if seen before it reaches the vessel, the terrified sailors can easily evade its approach."

Albertus M. Rondeletius * has also made mention of this fish in his book on the Monoceros, while there are many who have noticed it when writing on the subject of fishes. We may compare also Olearius, *Persian Journeys*, Bk. I. chap. 4, fol. 175.†

---

* William Rondelet was born at Montpellier in 1507, and practised medecine there. His principal work is :—A Treatise on Fish, 1554, 2 vols., folio. Rabelais is said to have satirised him under the name of *Rondibilis*. He died of a surfeit of figs in 1566.

† Adam Olearius was the son of a tailor of Steenwick in the Netherlands. He became secretary to the embassy sent by Frederick to the Czar and the Shah of Persia. The journey lasted six years, from 1633 to 1639. On his return, he wrote a history of his travels, as exact as it is detailed. He also issued a collection of stories, maxims, etc., drawn from Persian authors. He died in 1671, at the age of 68.

VI. Ælian (Bk. 17 of *History of Animals*, chap. 10), has introduced unicorns under the head of flying creatures. In the same way Duro, a writer of Persian history (as we learn from the Conon of Cornelius Nepos, and also from Athenaeus) mentions that unicorn-birds were found in Æthiopia. When Solimannus Eunuchus was bringing round his fleet to port, after having sailed over the Red Sea, there was seen on the coast of Portugal a unicorn-bird, a statement which is testified to by Lewis de Urreta, a monk of the Franciscan Order. *(History of Ethiopia*, p. 344.) The statement tendered by Thomas Bartholinus,* son of Caspard, page 50 of the book above quoted, is worthy of notice: "Rome, the mother of Nations, produced a basilisk ornamented with a single horn in its head, of the same appearance as the engraver has shewn in the woodcut. He, in fact, gives a picture of the creature.

VII. Among the many races of Reptiles, several cases, and these of an agreeable nature, could, by the exercise of diffuseness be quoted from Albertus Magnus† and Ulysses Aldrovandus.

---

*There were three writers named Bartholinus, Caspard, Thomas the elder, and Thomas the younger, father, son, and grandson. This is Thomas the elder.

†Thus called, not because he was really a great man, but because his family name was *Groot*, the

First of all however, we must quote that passage of John Veslingius * which is a source of wonder to the anatomists of our age. In this passage he states that in the suburbs of Cairo he had several times seen one-horned vipers of a most deadly nature. The Egyptians give them the name of Mamelukes or Regias, and say that Cleopatra, in times gone by, had applied them to her breasts.

Cardanus mentions a little worm in his book on subtilties, which springs from the leaves of the nightshade, which is marked by a green and yellow tinge, and carries a horn on its forehead, more than an inch in length. It is my opinion that Cardanus had confounded the mouth and what corresponds to the cartilage. The question is whether it has a horn, whence the animal may derive its name, or only some material, stiff and prickly, which by the lapse of time becomes transformed into cartilage. There is nothing new or wonderful in this; it happens to capons, or castrated cocks, as well as to this creature. Now shall we here delay long over the horned slug of Fabius Columna, which he calls by the name "Boucampe" or ox-foot, from its charac-

---

Dutch for great. He was born in 1205 and died in 1282. His works were collected in 1651, and form 21 large folio volumes.

* Veslingius died at Padua 1649. He was a celebrated anatomist.

teristic feature of being bent like the curved foot of an ox, and which is said by the Latins to be destructive to nuts.

VIII. Even among insects there are certain kinds furnished with only one horn. The species of beetles of this kind (not those double horned creatures which the German call Schröter) is admitted to be somewhat rare, and although less treated of by Authors, it is yet very common in Illyria. Next to Olaus of Worms, we must quote the words of Bartholinus, who was an eye-witness of the fact recorded and is a man of the greatest attainments. "When journeying between Salerno and Naples" he says "we came across a creature of the kind I have described. I have called it Unicorn, in opposition to the opinion of these most learned men Aldrovandus, and Imperatus, to whom it seems to be better described by the appellation Rhinoceros." But, dismissing these instances and that of the amphibious animal called the Camphor, we must call attention to quadrupeds, and enquire whether, perhaps, the vague meaning of the word may not be explained, as the result of petty mistakes and errors, more than anything else.

IX. In this branch of our subject such variety meets our view that I can no longer wonder at the fact that authors nowhere agree with one another in describing the nature of the monoceros.

This is the reason why many are suspicious of the stories told of the creature, why very many men are sceptical on the point, and more than one is reduced to a state of misgiving on the subject. For (1) there is said to be a one-horned ass or unicorn of India. This species is very often referred to by Pliny (Bk. ii., chap. 37, Nat. Hist.) and by Aristotle (Bk. ii., chap. 1; Bk. iii., chap. 2). And although Andreas Marinus, the sworn foe of the unicorn, considers this one-horned, one-footed creature in the light of a chimera, on the ground that none of the present generation of those who have travelled over the Indies, and other countries unknown to the ancients, have ever seen or heard of it, yet he is completely and fully refuted by Bartholinus (page 118).

X. Again, (2) the existence of one-horned horses is beyond all manner of doubt. It is only a very few years ago since the Elector of Saxony, the late John George I., of most glorious memory, was presented by a man named Kracchius (who had served his full term of military service in the Imperial army, and cannot be unknown to the inhabitants of Krackow) with a one-horned horse, which lost and renewed its horn annually. We shall here pass no remark on the testimony of Pliny, Strabo, and Solinus, since their authenticity is suspected by some (though we should remind these latter that accusation is quite a different thing from refutation). John Eusebius, of Nuremberg, a great authority, Professor of Physics at Madrid, in Spain (Nat. Hist., Bk. vii., chap. 2), says he saw, at the Court of Philip, a horned horse which had been brought from India. In the stables of the Prince of Sicily, Leo Allatius* saw a horse some years previously, of very meagre proportions, but of the greatest ferocity. This is on the testimony of Thomas Bartholinus.

XI. There are also oxen possessed of only one horn. Any one who pleases may consult Pliny, Bk. viii., chap. 21. His inconsistency, however, in at one time stating there are only Indian asses which are one-horned, and at another that there are oxen also, cannot be got over. Still, Ethiopia and India are the native places of this creature.

Caesar, also, in his "Gallic War," states that in the Hercynian Forest, oxen were to be found which had a kind of high straight horn in the middle of the forehead. It is moreover true that in some places cows with only one horn are reared. On this point we may quote Scaliger. He says: "In the same field as I mentioned above, at the town of Zeila, in Ethiopia, there are cows of a black colour, with stag's horns. I have called

---

* A native of Chios, who became Professor of Greek at Rome in 1600. He was afterwards Librarian to Cardinal Barberini, and later still, of the Vatican Library. He died in 1669, aged 83 years.

these creatures therefore "Cervines." Some have the horn in the middle of the forehead, and it forms a greater angle than the foot does with the leg, when at rest." Scaliger gives us the above statement on the authority of Lewis Vertomannus,* who saw, at the Sultan's court at Zeila, cows of the description given above. Under this head it may be well to bring the one-horned wild ox of Russia, which the Germans commonly term die Uhrochsen.† See, on this point, Erasmus Stela Bk. 1. Bartholinus, in his remarks on Ancient Russia, thinks these wild one-horned oxen to be

---

* Lewis Vertomannus was a Roman, who in 1503, undertook a voyage to the East. His extraordinary account of his journey was translated by Richard Eden in 1579, and reprinted by me for the *Aungervyle Society* (300 copies only) in 1884. The following is the passage referred to. It will be seen that either Kirchmayer or his authority, Scaliger, have somewhat misquoted Vertomannus. "There are also certaine kyne with hornes lyke vnto Hartes hornes, these are wylde; and when they bee taken, are giuen to the Soltan of that citie (Zeila) as a kyngly present. I sawe there also certayne kyne, hauing only one horne in the middest of the forehead, as hath the Vnicorne, and about a spanne of length, but the horne bendeth backwarde; they are of a bryght shynyng red colour. But they that haue hartes hornes, are enclynyng to blacke colour." (Bk. ii., Cap. 14. p. 94.)

† This is probably the "Urus" of Chancellor. (See *Bibliotheca Curiosa*; Chancellor's Voyage, p. 41.)

the same as those which Caesar says he saw wandering in the Hercynian forest.

XII. But we must not pass over without mention the one-horned oryx. The oryx, to explain the word, is so-called from its power of burrowing, either from a desire of being undisturbed, or because, from a petulant nature, like a boar, it digs up the earth, not with its head or mouth, but with its feet, with the intention of covering itself over with a blacker coating, so as not to see the rising sun or moon. The greatest divergence of opinion reigns as to what class of animals we are to refer the oryx to. Pliny (Bk. iii., chap. 37) and Columella (Bk. i., chap. 1) refer it to the deer, others to the ass tribe. However that may be, the oryx is a one-horned creature. Its habitat is Syria, Palestine, and Getulia, in Africa. We learn from Juvenal and Martial that it was considered a great delicacy. Juvenal writes:—

> *Et Scythiae volucres, et Phænicoplerus ingens,*
> *Et Getulus oryx.*

Martial, again, Bk. 13, Epigram 95 :—
> *Matutinarum non ultima praeda ferarum*
> *Saevus oryx constat quod mihi morte canum.*

The oryx has a very great power of withstanding thirst : its size is medium, and its colour very like that of the goat. The Kings of Egypt, in order to find out with accuracy the moment of sunrise were accustomed to mount the oryx, and make use of a wonderful horologue. I know, however, that the learned Salmasius * denies that the oryx, on account of the slimness of its body, can possibly support a rider. This point, however, we have nothing to do with here.

XIII. The rhinoceros is now, if I mistake not, the only subject left to deal with. The term itself, and the confusion of it with the monoceros, must be explained. Rhinoceros is derived from *rhinos*, a snout, and *keras* (cornu) a horn. This horn grows from its nose, and is a most deadly weapon, and the mortal dread of the elephant. Hence captious persons, who are very ready to blame others, and find fault with everything, are said to have a rhinoceros's nose. (See Martial, Bk. i., Epig. 3.)

The rhinoceros, though somewhat lower than the elephant in stature, and shorter in length, is yet his match. It has a divided hoof, a hide the colour of box-wood, and is protected by a double fold of this covering (I use the words of Camerarius,† Book i., chap. 25), "which, like a solid breast-plate, forms an impenetrable shield." It is

---

* The well-known opponent of Milton.

† This is Camerarius the younger, born 1534, died 1598. Besides works on natural history and botany, he wrote a Life of Melancthon, 1655, 8vo.

armed with a horn of bone like its hoof, placed on its snout, with which its custom is to strike and pierce the belly of the elephant, its irreconcilable enemy. Nature has placed an insurmountable antipathy between the rhinoceros and the elephant. In the year of Grace 1513, May 1st, one was brought to the King of Portugal. This king, two years after, for the sake of making a show at Ulyssipona, let this creature and an elephant loose together, and the Rhinoceros came off victorious. This is so much an ascertained fact that it is quite beyond the possibility of doubt.

(See Paulus Jovius, Cardanus, book x. folio 328, Scaliger, exercitation, 205, section 1. Franzius, and also Thomas Bartholinus, on the Unicorn, amongst the addenda on page 147.) In the 43rd chapter of Suetonius, we are told the same thing of Octavius Augustus. Hence those that deny it, deny it in vain. In 1515, a Portuguese knight, Damianus à Goës, saw a like spectacle at the same place, in the reign of King Emmanuel.

XIV. Care must be taken, however, not to confound the Rhinoceros with the Monoceros, a mistake the student of ancient times frequently falls into. Scaliger accuses Cardanus of this same mistake (Exerc. 205, sec. 1.), in these words. "Of what ill destiny are you the victim, that in spite of the frequent castigations you receive from the rod of the grammarians, you should now fall under the censure of the naturalists? You are past any help, Cardanus, when you describe the monoceros under the heading of rhinoceros, although these creatures are quite distinct." Such are the words of Scaliger, a man for whom we have as much reverence as the great Conqueror of the world had for his own Home; for, in my opinion there is no thinker more deep or more accurate than Scaliger. Although, then, I wish his memory every good, I cannot defend him in the present instance. There is no doubt he has thrown an undeserved slur on Cardanus, who has taken quite the opposite view to that here imputed to him. (Bk. x., folio 326 ; Basle, H. Peter's Edition.) For after giving a definition of the rhinoceros, and clearing the way for the connection between it and the monoceros, he makes the following interpolation :—" It is clear that this creature (*i.e.*, the rhinoceros, of which he was till then speaking) is quite distinct from the monoceros, with which its only relation is a similarity of name." Unless, perhaps, Scaliger really has in his mind some other passage of Cardanus, which I can nowhere find in his works.

XV. Up to this point we have considered many kinds of monoceros, though using the term rather as an adjective than a noun. Now, after our general statement about one-horned animals, we have still to investigate what, *par excellence*, was meant to be implied by what the Latins called *unicornu*, the Greeks *monoceros*, the Hebrew *r,em*, the Germans 𝕮𝖆𝖌 𝕺𝖎𝖓𝖍𝖔𝖗𝖓, the French *lycorne*, the Italians *alicorno* and *lioncorno*, and other nations by other names. Now, therefore, we have to investigate what the unicorn is, where it exists, and the qualities with which it is endowed. This we proceed to do.

END OF VOL. I.

Printed by E. & G. Goldsmid, Edinburgh.

[COLLECTANEA ADAMANTÆA.—XV.]

Un=Natural History,

OR

Myths

OF

ANCIENT SCIENCE;

Being a Collection of Curious Tracts on the
Basilisk, Unicorn, Phœnix, Behemoth or
Leviathan, Dragon, Giant Spider,
Tarantula, Chameleons, Satyrs,
Homines Caudati,
&c.

NOW FIRST TRANSLATED FROM
THE LATIN,

AND

Edited, with Notes and Illustrations,

BY

EDMUND GOLDSMID, F.R.H.S.,
F.S.A. (Scot.)

IN FOUR VOLUMES.

VOL. II.

PRIVATELY PRINTED.
EDINBURGH.
1886.

[COLLECTANEA ADAMANTÆA.]

Myths of Ancient Science.

This Reprint is limited to 275 small-paper and 75 large-paper copies.

[COLLECTANEA ADAMANTÆA. XV.]

Un=Natural History,

OR

MYTHS

OF

ANCIENT SCIENCE;

Being a Collection of Curious Tracts on the Basilisk, Unicorn, Phœnix, Behemoth or Leviathan, Dragon, Giant Spider, Tarantula, Chameleons, Satyrs, Homines Caudati, &c.

NOW FIRST TRANSLATED FROM THE LATIN,

AND

Edited, with Notes and Illustrations.

BY

EDMUND GOLDSMID, F.R.H.S.,
F.S.A. (Scot.)

IN FOUR VOLUMES.

VOL. II.

PRIVATELY PRINTED.
EDINBURGH.
1886.

The Unicorn—*Continued.*

CHAPTER II.
CONTENTS.

1. Definition of unicorn.
2. God himself has implanted the indomitable ferocity of the unicorn in it. It is a solitary animal. The testimony of Idaith Aga a Turkish writer, examined.
3. The unicorn praised by God himself for its courage and speed.
4. It is an inhabitant of Arabia, Syria, Tartary, Ethiopia, and India. Two unicorns seen at Mecca by the great Vertomannus. Many of them kept by the King of Persia.
5. An account of the size, shape, bodily habits, and sounds produced by the Monoceros.
6. The petty disputes of some writers passed over. Reason given. Vertomannus excused and reconciled.
7. The existence of the Monoceros confirmed by arguments.
8. The unicorn not without good authorities. At Dresden, a unicorn on constant view. At Fredericksburg, in Denmark, two unicorns seen by Aldrovandus.
9. The side of experience, sense, and historical truthfulness is to be taken by us.
10. The fable of the extinction of the unicorn at the Flood refuted.
11. Is the unicorn an antidote for all poisons.
12. How the true may be distinguished from the false unicorn horn.
13. Note to the reader.

I. The unicorn (of which we are at present speaking) is a four-footed animal, with a single and very long horn on its forehead. The creature is incapable of being tamed, of a very fierce, solitary, and brave temperament, and possesses extraordinary speed. It is an inhabitant of the wild wastes of Arabia, Syria, Ethiopia, and India. It is of the size of a horse, and has that creature's mane. It has the feet, head, and legs of a stag, and the tail of a goat or hog. Its cry is of the most terrible description.

Of the form of the animal, as of everything else with the exception of man, we are, *à priori*, ignorant. Accordingly, the definition we give is merely an enumeration of certain peculiar properties and distinctive marks, and is, at the same time, somewhat vague. We proceed as best we can, not as we ought, for that is impossible. That it is an animal, a quadruped, and carries a single horn on its forehead, is devoid of all doubt. On the nature and value of this horn we shall speak further on, in some notes to our main treatise. What follows requires the corroboration of proof.

II. We have used the words "incapable of being tamed," and "of a very fierce nature." God himself said this. In Job, chap. xxxix., v. 9-10, we read—"Will the unicorn" (*N.B.*—Some incorrectly substitute *rhincceros* here and elsewhere for *unicorn* in translating the Hebrew *r,em*, but against them we have not only Luther, but the Septuagint, and French, Italian, Spanish, English, and Belgian translators, to say nothing of Drusius, Schlinder, Flacius, and others) "Will the unicorn be willing to serve thee, or abide by thy crib? Canst thou bind the unicorn with his band in the furrow? or will he harrow the valleys after thee?" Hence in Psalm xxii., verse 21, the cruel persecutors of our Lord are not inaptly compared to unicorns, and placed by the side of the lion. The Messiah complains thus :—"Save me from the lion's mouth: for thou hast heard me from the horns of the unicorns."

That it is a solitary animal is clear from many proofs. It is an infallible truth of zoology that all creatures of a fierce disposition, such as the lion, leopard, panther, and bear, delight in solitude. Special points to be noted are that it inhabits untrodden tracts and districts furthest removed from the haunts of man. With very few exceptions it has never come into the possession of man, unless in the sense that its horns, when cast, are sometimes found. The rarity of these horns makes them coveted and dear. This is my reason for believing that Idaith Aga (an Ambassador of Solyman at the Court of the Emperor Maximilian, known as Marcus Scherer before his abjuration of the Christian religion, and a great friend of Ulysses Aldrovandus) did not take the word unicorn in its peculiar and distinctive sense, when he dared to say in a full meeting of the first men of Vienna that he had seen these animals in a desert part of Arabia, wandering about in flocks like herds of cattle.

III. Its courage is shown forth by God himself to Job in the book called after him, chapter xxxix. v. 11, "Wilt shou trust him because his strength is great?" and in Numbers, chap. xxiii, v. 22, "God hath brought them out of Egypt; he hath as it were the strength of an unicorn." The same words exactly, occur again in chapter xxiv. 8. We maintain that the speed of the unicorn is not inferior to that of the goat, panther, hare, horse, or dog. Psalm xxix, 6, is especially noteworthy, where we read that Jehovah "makes the cedars of Lebanon to skip like a young unicorn."* Any creature may be possessed of extreme speed, when it is not overburdened with a mass of flesh. Indeed among both men and the lower animals, the strong are the swift.

IV. That it is an inhabitant of Arabia and Syria requires no further proof than that in very many passages of Sacred Writ it is made an inhabitant of Phœnicia, Syria, and Arabia. These animals, accordingly, were not altogether unknown. A clearer proof of this may be got, I believe, from Psalm xxix, 6, where it is said: "Thou maketh

---

* This verse is misquoted. In the authorised version it reads: "He maketh them (the cedars) skip like a calf; Lebanon and Sirion like a young Unicorn."

them (that is, the cedars) to skip like a calf;
Lebanon and Sirion like a young unicorn." Here
it is conjoined with Lebanon and Sirion in a sort
of treble comparison and in a following verse*
with the wilderness of Kadesh. From these
quotations, I believe, the argument holds good
that in this case the thing contained has some
relation to the thing containing it (*i.e.* the Unicorn
to the wilderness of Kedesh, Lebanon, or Sirion.)
We have the authority of the most unimpeachable
authorities for saying that it is an inhabitant of the
the wilds of Ethiopia and India. Lewis Vertomannus, of Bologna, whom Scaliger speaks of as
an excellent man in his 205th Discursus, saw two
unicorns at Mecca, which, he says, were sent over
by the Prince of Ethiopia as the means of cement-
ing a closer friendship with the Sultan.† M.

* The 8th.

† The passage alluded to is as follows : " On the
other part of the temple are parkes or places inclosed,
where are seene two Vnicorns, named of the Greekes
Monocerotæ, and are there shewed to the people for
a myracle, and not without good reason, for their
seldomenesse and strange nature. The one of them,
which is much hygher then the other, yet not much
vnlike to a coolte of thyrtye moneths of age, in the
forehead groweth only one horne, in maner ryght
foorth, of the length of three cubites. The other is
much younger, of the age of one yeere, and lyke a
young coolte, the horne of this is of the length of
foure handfuls. This beast is of the coloure of a

Paulus Venetus,* from his long acquaintance with the Tartars, and more especially the Eastern tribes of them, (Bk. iii. chap. 15, on Oriental writings) says that unicorns and elephants are found in great numbers in that country. Similarly Leonard Ranchwolff writes to the effect that he had heard from a certain Persian, that the Sophy, King of Persia, brought up two or three unicorns at Samarcand. Thomas Bartholinus, in the passage quoted above, says: "Sailors and merchants who have returned to Europe from China

---

horse of weesell coloure, and hath the head lyke an hart, but no long necke, a thynne mane hangyng onlye on the syde ; theyr legges are thyn and slender lyke a fawne or hynde ; the hoofes of the fore feet, are diuided in two, much like the feet of a goat, the outwarde part of the hynder feete is very full of heare. This beast doubtlesse seemeth wylde and fierce, yet tempereth that fiercenesse with a certain comelinesse. These Vnicornes one gaue to the Soltan of Mecha, as a most precious and rare gyfte. They were sent hym out of Ethiope by a kyng of that countrey, who desired by that present to gratifie the Soltan of Mecha." (Voyages of Vertomannus in 1503, translated by Richard Eden in 1576, and reprinted for the Aungervyle Society 1884. Series III. pp. 56-57.)

* Or Marco Polo. He was a Venetian by birth and travelled in Tartary with his father and uncle. On his return to Italy in 1295, he wrote an account of his journey and seventeen years' residence at the court of the Grand Khan, which was first printed at Venice in 1495, 8vo.

and other districts of India* bear witness to this fact. They say that when traversing the vast deserts with cautious footsteps, they have seen, in the deserts of Arabia and other solitary places, a wild beast of this description take refuge in woods and untrodden places, and not without a feeling of fear in their own hearts. But so great was its speed, they say, that it very quickly was lost to view, and prevented those who saw it from obtaining a more accurate look at it."

V. The other points, namely, those that concern its size, shape, and habit of body and cry, we shall now consider shortly, in order to make our work as brief as possible. We are not however without proofs. After Cardanus, from whom we have above quoted a passage, we must give an extract from Scaliger, which is to the following effect :— "Unicorns are about the size of a horse; they have the head, feet, and legs of a stag, their hair and coat is of a dark chesnut tinge. They have the mane of a horse, though scantier and not so long. Their hips are covered with hair. I have seen a horn of one of these creatures at Nicea, and others at different places. One of these was yellowish, another of a dull tinge, more like the

---

* China *and other* districts of India ! Bartholinus may have been very learned, but he certainly was no Geographer.

colour of box than anything else. Another was reddish. I have a piece of one in my possession, which is of a white colour." Its cry Ælian describes as most unearthly and shrill; Pliny says it is a deep bellow, while Solinus calls it terrible. The words of the late Sperlingius, in his *Lectures on Zoology* (On the Unicorn, cap. vi., part 7), apply in this instance. "The cry of this animal cannot be exactly described apart from other cries." Eusebius says:—"The cry of the cat and unicorn is disgusting, and has a weird ring about it. There is no doubt about the cry of the cat. Their cries vary with their different wants. When goaded by desire they give forth unearthly cries, and fill a house with their loud yells."*

VI. After what has been said on this point, we pass on to the common tradition, which has not been unopposed by authorities, as to the hoofs, feet, horn, and similar adjuncts of the unicorn. Some, for instance, say its hoof is solid, others that it is cleft. Some declare its feet are hairy, others that they are soft and smooth. Some say its horn is of the length of two cubits, others that it is more or less; and while some say the colour of this horn is dusky grey, and others black or dusky, there are even some who maintain it is of a bright hue. These points, however, are of too

---

* A fact that can be sworn to by millions

minor importance to require a detailed discussion. The individual varies with the locality. We can see one kind of dog in England, another in Germany, though both are of the same species. And without further words, we may say that the variety of the human race is so great that a comparison of Germans with Ethiopians, of these with Italians, of Italians with Danes, Greenlanders, Laplanders, or Muscovites, would be a source of great surprise to us. In the meantime, however, are we to admit that the unicorn is a peaceable creature in the sense that Scaliger and Vertomannus do?* I, of course, agree with the Scriptures, and experience of other men, who attribute to it unsatiable ferocity; but are we to side with Bartholinus, and say that some small corruption has crept into the text of Vertomannus? Had we, however, any reason to offer for the statement of either of these authorities, we would say that the two unicorns which were seen by Vertomannus had been tamed by a long captivity and subjection, whereby their otherwise unconquerable ferocity had been completely crushed out. There is no doubt that this is the case with lions, bears, and panthers, the fiercest of the animal creation.

VII. Such being the case, who cares any longer

---

* Vertomannus says nothing of the kind; see extract given p. 9, note.

to be of such simplicity or obstinacy as not to hestitate to oppose his own view to so many proofs, both divine and human, for the existence of the unicorn? Who does not dread to do so? The sacred writings speak out on the subject, and in many places praise the unicorn. Shall we now stand up, and contend for the non-existence of the Unicorn? Nature herself complains, and is loud in her own defence, while from time to time she urges that the Creator of the world was not so utterly careless of the animal creation at the time of the impending Flood, as these writers try to make out. The power of procreation was not given them for no purpose. Though the individual dies, the species certainly survives. "If," says the acute Scaliger, "anything were wanting, a vacuum would be created in the forms of animal life. This would be a far greater fault in Nature, than a vacuum in space without substance." We have already fully seen how many are the species of unicorns. Lewis Vertomannus saw two unicorns called such, par excellence. This man, two centuries ago, made a minute examination of the whole of the East, both Egypt and the two Arabias, Africa, and India, as the journal of his whole journeys clearly shews. "This Vertomannus" (I use the words of Bartholinus) "on coming to Meccha, a great city in the Arabian desert, accompanied by his companions in his journey, went first over the celebrated temple of Mahomet. Having turned to one side of this temple he saw two creatures which he recognised as unicorns. This is testified to by his own words." (Bk. I. cap. 18, "On Arabia.")*

VIII. Is there any Prince, Duke, or King in the world, who has not either seen, or possessed and regarded as among the most precious of his possessions, a unicorn's horn? The Dresden *exotikothaumatourgematatameion*,† a word which, though confused, is yet ingenious, and is used by Vechnerus, in his breviary or description of Germany, certainly is not without a specimen. There is also in Fredricksburg (the finest fortified town of the King of Denmark) a unicorn's horn, seven feet in length (Roman measure), and with a girth of seven inches. It is a conspicuous object, and has been described by D. Thomas Bartholinus, a Dane. Ulysses Aldrovandus, a man of the widest reading, in his discussions on quadrupeds (Bk. I., page 223), says, "I have seen at Rome two unicorns' horns, one which belonged to Pope Clement VII., and another, which was the property of my own nephew, the very famous prince Peter, Cardinal Aldrovandus, &c."

---

* Poor Kirchmayer! How would he account for the numerous extinct species now known only from their bones, the Mastodous, Megatheriums, &c.

† Now the Museum.

IX. To Historians we must either grant historical accuracy, or the fact must be proved more fully by our own efforts. Where, in truth, are we, if history does not stand on its own legs? Certain mad Thomists* may now come and try to cry me down by bringing up at one time the difference of opinion existing among some authors when describing this animal; at another, some empty argument or other. My answer is a short one. I do not listen to them. The words of a very learned man, Aldrovandus (Nat. Hist. Quad. Bk. I. cap. 6), are worth quoting. "Those to whose minds my answers are lacking in trustworthiness, I maintain, are wanting in intellect, and I call them obstinate who do not blush to deny the evidence of their senses, since so many proofs of the existence of the unicorn are everywhere apparent." It is my opinion, nevertheless, that many of these specimens have been obtained more from desert places, than as the actual results of hunting. The horns are those that have fallen, and can easily be distinguished from other horns by their general appearance, colour, size, and shape.

---

* From this we may rank Kirchmayer as a Scotist. The Thomists and Scotists represented the rival orders of the Dominicans and Franciscans. Their theological disputes lasted for centuries. The names refer to their leaders, Thomas Aquinas and Duns Scotus.

X. But at this point we must once for all destroy that error, which is firmly fixed in many minds. It is said that these animals perished at the great flood, and that their bones are now dug up from the earth. But it is a fact, which must be a source of joy and congratulation to vendors of trifles, that this is a kind of mineral,* which neither by its hardness, nor weight, nor solidity, nor scent, has anything in common with the horn we are discussing, not to speak of several of its higher properties.

It is dug up in Thuringia, Bohemia, the Hercynian Forest near Elbingerod, at Hildesheim, Heidelberg, in Silesia, Moravia, and many places of Misnia. Clusius, Ferrantes Imperatus (Bk. 25), and Franciscus, his son, mention that it is found in Italy. Olaus Wormius possesses several pieces, one of which, on the authority of Bartholinus, is white, friable, soft, and of a very agreeable scent. Sennertus makes a true remark when he says:— "Why is it more likely that these horns should be found in some places rather than others in which the unicorn lived?"

XI. In order, however, to separate the gold from the dross and the true from the false, we propose to place two minor questions in the

---

* This passage is far from clear, but evidently refers to those stones, mentioned in Vol. I., p. 54, as being a cure for broken limbs, ulcers, &c.

B

appendix, which will help us. One question is to the following effect:—Is the unicorn horn a cure for all diseases, or does it possess, even in the slightest degree, those virtues which are attributed to it? I answer:—The world is prone to be deceived. No man does an injury willingly. A just man goes to extremes occasionally. Rumour is but an echo; it doubles and trebles everything. Many things are said in praise of great men to win their favour. Poisons are of such varied natures that it is impossible for a single antidote to be given for them all. Men exaggerate everything by their individual treatment of rumour. Deceit is rampant in market places and such like haunts of men. The greatest doctors among the Arabians, Ethiopians, Greeks or Latins would not have been struck dumb at these most divine properties. Nothing is now praised except what comes from the Indies and the Malay islands. Every-day events, although of the greatest importance, pass unnoticed from constant repetition.* A most learned writer, D. Thomas Bartholinus, quotes Crato of Crafithem, Baccius, Horatius, Augenius Horstius

---

* It is not easy to see what all this has to do with the question proposed : *Is the Uuicorn's horn a cure for all diseases ?* It reads rather like the celebrated " What ! no soap ! So he died, and she, very imprudently, married the barber, etc. etc."

and others, and declares that the horn of the stag and the horn of the rhinoceros are every whit as good as the unicorn's. The same decision is come to by Aldrovandus, by Andreas Marinus and Apollonius.

XII. How can the true unicorn's horn be distinguished from the false? The answer given is: If, when thrown into hot water it causes bubbles to rise; if, when poison is present, it produces perspiration; if it heals dogs that have drunk of poison; if, by means of this horn, a circle may be drawn in which a lizard, scorpion, or spider being placed, it does not attempt to retreat. In all this, however, superstition and truth strive for the mastery. It is false that the 'unicorn' horn sweats, that it is the only thing that can always cause bubbles in hot water. The account which Jordanus gives of a certain Jew and other beggars,* is merely a result of superstition and magic, for these men used magical incantations to prevent their spiders, serpents and scorpions from crossing a drawn line, and did not work with the help of a unicorn's horn. If there is any substratum of truth in the statement; it is not by a circle, but certain hidden qualities of which it is an allegory, that they

---

* Jordanus says a Jew and his companions drew a circle with Unicorn Horn, whence no reptile could escape.

produced the effects they did. Bartholinus, in chapter 10, and in what he says on several occasions, agrees with us, when he calls this account the greatest nonsense. Meanwhile we are safe in saying that no one denies that the unicorn's horn is an antidote to poison.

NOTE TO THE READER.

XIV. I ask for these lines a kindly reading. To the good, all things are good; to the wicked, the best things appear the worst. I have undertaken this writing by the advice of friends. I am, on the present occasion, indebted to many wise men, to whom I bear a most humble sense of reverence. To Bartholinus, son of Casparus, a man of the greatest distinction, I am under the greatest obligation, and own it with pleasure. I neither could, nor ought to have spurned the stories alluded to herein of my own consciousness. Bartholinus's lot it was to do that before me. I have on every occasion, however, used my own talents in discriminating, and have not given a hasty credence to every chance promiscuous tale. An impartial reader will see this, and if I have done anything amiss, he will impute it to me; if anything good, to God, to whom alone be glory everlasting.

AMEN.

On the Phœnix,

BY

GEORGE CASPARD KIRCHMAYER.

PREFACE.

WHAT is scarce is prized. Poets are not the only sources of profit and pleasure. Philosophers are so too. I, who am the lowest and last of the learned, claim none of these qualities for myself. Could there be, indeed, a more immodest claim than such a one on my part? Yet while the result I come to may be a very small one, I take credit for the attempt as being a praiseworthy one. A year ago I held a dissertation on the Basilisk, while quite recently the Unicorn was the subject of my investigations. On another occasion I ˄shall treat of the behemoth and leviathan if spared. At the present time I propose to enquire into the subject of the Phœnix. I do so, in order to bring together the great number of similitudes, proverbs, phenomena, and remarks which have been made on this subject, and which are found collected nowhere else. I have to enquire, with the help of God, what real truth there is in the Phœnix.

On the Phœnix.

CHAPTER I.

ARGUMENT.

1. The term Phœnix. The palm, its nature.
2. Notes on the accentuation of the word.
3. Explanation of different meanings of the term.
4. The Phœnicians, not the first seamen, nor the discoverers of letters.
5 and 6. Different meanings of the term, continued.
7. Synonyms of the word.
8. A description of the Phœnix as given by mythologists.
9. Varied and incredible reports as to its longevity.
10. Supposed to be the only specimen of its kind in the world. A quotation from Clement, of Rome.
11. Said to rise again from its own ashes. Manner thereof.
12. A curious and more exact statement of the circumstances, by Clement, of Rome.
13. The materials from which it is re-born a matter of dispute among authors.
14. Its locality and birth-place. It is supposed to have been an inhabitant of Paradise by Lactantius Firmianus.
15. Men of the greatest authority have rejected the notion of the story being a myth, and accepted it as an historical fact. Their names.
16. Estimate of Clement's evidence.

I. No one can rightly estimate what he knows nothing about. The blind are thus in the habit of forming opinions about colours. In order to conduct our enquiry in good faith, I shall first speak of those things that are everywhere mentioned by authors on the mythical subject of the Phœnix, and then shall proceed in order to the full discussion of the whole subject. To begin, then, with the word itself. The term "phœnix" is so called, according to Pliny, from the palm tree, because the bird is of a bright purple colour. It need not be mentioned that the Greeks call the palm "phœnix." Judæa and the whole of Syria are very abundant in palm trees. This is proved by the Holy Scriptures, and by Pliny, when speaking of the palm trees of Syria (Bk. 13, c. 5). Pliny's words in his description of the palm tree are very well chosen. He says—"In many places this tree is used as a kind of rough coat, as it were, to protect the walls of houses against damp. The palms of greater height form whole forests, the trunks of the tree being protected all round by pointed leaves, which are arranged in the form of a comb; these are, it must be understood, wild palms, though sometimes by some wayward fancy or other they are known to make their appearance among the cultivated varieties. The other kinds are tall, round, and tapering, and, being furnished with dense projecting knobs or circles in the bark, arranged in regular gradation, they are found easy of ascent by the people in the East; in order to do which the climber fastens a loop of osier round his body and the trunk, and by this contrivance ascends the tree with great speed. All the foliage is at the summit, and the fruit as well; this last being situate not among the leaves, as is the case with other trees, but hanging in clusters from roots of their own among the branches, and partaking of the nature both of the grape and apple. The leaves terminate in a sharp point like that of a knife, while the sides, being deeply indented, were first looked upon as lovely gems. At the present day they are split open to form ropes and wythes for fastening, as well as light umbrellas for covering the head."

II. There is another explanation of the name found in Isidorus (Bk. xii., chap. 7). "The Arabians," he says, "call anything out of the ordinary, 'phœnix,' and the phœnix is a singular and unique creation among the feathered tribes." This, however, has little to do with our subject. We must make a note on the accentuation of the word. $\phi o\iota\nu\iota\xi$ has the vowel iota short, though by position it would be long, while in all the other cases except the vocative it is long by nature. Eustathius is our authority on this point. Wellerus says that in $\phi o\iota\nu\iota\xi$, $\theta\omega\rho a\xi$, $\kappa\grave{\eta}\rho\upsilon\xi$ and in all such words the last syllable is by nature long, as is seen in the genitive. (Greek Grammar 'On Accents,' rule 3, p. 60.) Pasor in his tract on accentuation, rule 12, recognises in this, as in similar instances, an exception to the general usage. For this reason we shall accuse no one.

III. To prevent our confounding truth with error, or rejecting it altogether, we must remove all ambiquity from the term. The word Phœnix is commonly accepted as meaning reddish (being used as an adjective), or something very nearly approaching red. An instance of this occurs in Apoll. Argent. 2., which, being translated, means "The helmet shone with ruddy plume." It is also commonly used as a substantive. (1) As the name of a man. Thus in Homer's Iliad, Bk. i., the tutor of Achilles is called Phœnix. The son of Antenor the Trojan, and brother of Cadmus, was also called by this name. Orosius, however, says that Cadmus was the son of Amyndor. The matter is of little importance here. In Pliny, a certain Phœnix, the disciple of Lysippus, a statuary, is mentioned, Bk. xxxiv., chap. 8. In Pausanias (in his Itinerary of Greece), we hear of a certain poet whose name was Phœnix. Those who have dipped deeply into mythological lore tell us that Phœnix was the son of Neptune and Lybia. From him, or perhaps from the brother of Cadmus, the national name of Phœnicians has sprung. We know the verse of Silius—

Et qui longa dedit terris cognomina Phoenix.

IV. How great was the wondrous genius of the Phœnicians that enabled them to excel all the rest of the world! They are considered by most men to have invented letters, and to have been the first to discover the art of navigation. Let me quote Dionysius—

> Phœnicum regio est : hi rubro gurgite quondam
> Mutavere domum, primique per æquora vecti,
> Lustravere salum, primi docuere carinis
> Ferre cavis, orbis commercia—

Also Lucan, Bk. iii.—

> Phœnices primi (famæ si creditur) ausi
> Mansuram rudibus vocem signare figuris.

While I do not deny that the Phœnicians were the most skilful mariners, and were especially pre-eminent in their study of the mathematical science, I yet maintain that they were not the first of mankind to discover the art of navigation and of letters. For what in such a case becomes of Noah to whom, and to whose posterity as a natural consequence, the Creator himself imparted the skill of navigation?* On this point we are opposed by Simon † (Major. in Dieb. canicul. coll.

---

* Our author seems here to suggest that Noah had something to do with the navigating of the ark. If so, I fear he must have come into collision with the orthodox believers in Scripture, almost as much as the late Doctor Colenso, who dared to express a doubt as to the very existence of that floating menagerie.

† Richard Simon, born at Dieppe in 1638, died

23, p. 796), by Andrew Senftleben, and recently by Loccenius,* Bk. i., chap. I., On Maritime and Naval Law. (Thesis. ii. p. 10.) To the Hebrews, again, and the Sacred People of God, we are to attribute the custody of letters rather than to the Phœnicians. The sound shews this to be the case: it is attested by the sense of order: a healthy and reasoning mind is satisfied with nothing else: the sacred writings themselves demand it. This, however, by the way.†

V. Again (2), a certain horse belonging to Cleosthenis Epidamnus was called Phœnix. (3) Pausanias has recorded that a river of Thessalia, which emptied itself into the Asopus, bore the name of Phœnix (Pliny, Bk. iv., cap. 9; Strabo, Bk. ix.). There is also another which flows through the Ægian territory and falls into the sea, as again Pausanius declares in his "Itinerary." (4) There is also a mountain of the same name, the highest in all the neighbouring region, and on which there was once a citadel standing. It is

---

there in 1712. He was a priest of much learning, and wrote a number of curious works more or less connected with religious questions.

* John Loccenius was one of the professors at the University of Upsala in 1670. His most curious work is *Leges West Gothicæ*, folio.

† Kirchmayer, as we know, has been proved to be wrong.

situate in the southward direction, and close to the Isthmus of the Dorian Chersonesus. This isthmus, however, many authorities do not recognise as the Chersonesus, for it is the Peleponnesus, as Stephanus warns us (Strabo, Bk, xiv., Æn. Sylv. On Asia Minor, cap. 87). (5) There is also a certain plant thus named, which is very commonly found by road sides, the flower of which is very like the darnel (I use the words of Aldrovandus), whence it is also called wood-darnel (Dioscoris Bk. iv., cap. 39; Pliny, Bk. xxii., cap. 25).

VI. (6) Several of the ancient astrologers did (I speak on the authority of Hyginus) call the Little Bear constellation by the name Phœnix. The reason no doubt was that Thales (who was the first to call that constellation Arctoa) was by birth a Phoenician. There is another of the Southern constellations which has recently been discovered by sailors, a star of which is known by this name. (7) We have noticed above that the palm tree was called the phœnix by the Greeks. (8) There is also a kind of dye which gets the name of Phœnician.* (9) A certain musical instrument also which was invented by the Phoenicians gets the same name. Of this Athenæus speaks in his fourteenth book. (10) Phœnix is also said to denote the Elizir of Life by Aldrovandus, (Bk.

---

* The purple of Tyre.

12. Ornith, chap. 27.) Nay, (11) the word also signifies an ointment or eye salve, as we are told by Stephanus in his Greek and Latin Lexicon. But (12) by far its principal meaning is that of the mythical bird with which we have stated it is our present purpose to deal.

VII. The synonyms of this term are many and varied. Claudian calls the phœnix par excellence the long-lived bird (Bk. 2) for speaking of the Rape of Proserpine he says:—

> Quicquid ab extremis longæva colonis
> Colligit, optatæ referens exordia vitæ.

Again, Ovid (2 Amor. El. 6), always calls it the Unique Bird.

> Et vivax Phœnix unica semper avis.

In Textor it has the following names:—The bird of second birth, the Pharian bird, long-lived, tenacious of life, the bird of the Ganges, of Assyria, the bird of the sun, of Titania, of Incense and of Fire. By the French it is called Phœnix, by the Italians Fenice, by the Spaniards Fenix, by the Germans der Vogel Fenix. But let us now return to the matter in hand.

VIII. According to painters and poets, the Phœnix is a bird of very large size, and of great beauty, very tenacious of life, being the only specimen in the whole creation of neither sex, and suddenly re-appearing from its own ashes.

We shall consider the Phœnix part by part, and shall enquire into those various qualities which are commonly attributed to it by credulity or superstition. In the first place, let us explain or enquire into its size. It is said to be equal in size to the eagle. Herodotus, in that book of his histories which goes under the name of Euterpe, not only claims for it a size equal to the eagle, but declares that it is similar to that bird in every bodily characteristic. This, however, he draws, not from his own, but from others' experience. Philostratus, on the authority of Tzeze (Bk. v. Hist. Chiliad. 6), writes that it is larger than the peacock, and so differs very little from Herodotus. Next, as to its beauty. Lactantius Firmianus, than whom there is not a greater fanatic on this point, (to use a strong term), has written a complete poem which he has called "Phœnix." He says:—

> Mitia quem croceo Punica grana legunt,
> Hoc humeri, pectusque decens, velamine fulgent :
> Hoc caput, hoc cervix, summaque terga nitent.
> Caudaque porrigitur fulvo distincta metallo.
> In cujus maculis purpura mista rubet.
> Clarum inter pennas insigne est ; desuper iris,
> Pingere ceu nubem desuper alta solet.
> Æquatur toti capiti radiata, corona :
> Phœbei referens verticis alta, decus.
> Effigies inter Pavonis mista figuram
> Cernitur, et mistam Phasidis inter avem.

IX. Next as to its longevity. Writers vary on this point more than on any other, so many are the varied forms which falsehood presents. Cornelius Tacitus writes:—Many different accounts are given of the number of years the Phœnix lives. A space of five hundred years is the most common acceptation. Pliny gives 660 as the number, Herodotus and Mela 540, Philostratus 600, Seneca 500, Albertus 350. To minds steeped in superstition such an age as this could not have seemed too great, had not Chæremon, the Egyptian, and other six poets (whose privilege it is to talk nonsense) given more than 7000 years as the years of the life of the Phœnix. Ovid is more reasonable, and in the 15th Book of his *Metamorphoses* he has spoken the ordinary sentiment of men—

Hæc ubi quinque suæ complevit secula vitæ
Ilicis in ramis, tremulaque cacumine palmæ,
Unguibus et duro nidum sibi construit ore, etc.

"Longer lived than a Phœnix" has become a proverb. Oppian has brought forward a reason for the long life of this bird when he says that it cannot be killed by arrows, stones, or by the other contrivances of man.

X. It is commonly said that the Phœnix is the only bird of its kind in the whole world, and accordingly it is of neither gender. This, at least, is what we read in the lately-discovered manuscript—I mean the letter of Clement of Rome to the Corinthians. What value is to be attached to this we shall hereafter enquire. "Let us consider the wonderful marvel which is found in Eastern countries and in Arabia. It is a bird which is called the Phœnix; this creature is the only one of its kind, is solitary in its life, and lives for 500 years."

Lactantius says:—

Fœmina vel mas hæc, vel neutrum sit mage felix,
Felix, quæ Veneris fœdera nulla colit
Mors illi Venus est, sola est in morte voluptas
Ut poscit nasci hæc, appetit ante mori.

Also, the bard of Mantua* sings—

Sola inter volucres, nec mas nec fœmina, sexu.
Sola caret, veneris sola adversatur honores.

Hence there has arisen a dispute among grammarians as to the gender of this bird, which belongs to neither sex. But such a discussion is merely a case of splitting hairs.

XI. No one who worships this idol of the poets denies that the Phœnix springs to life from its own ashes. Pliny, who himself regards the Phœnix in the light of a myth, quotes from Manilius (Bk. x., chap. 2, *Natural History*). "The best account of all has been given by Manilius, a Senator, and the most active of state officers. This man, who has become famous in the deepest sciences without

---

* Virgil.

any teacher, says that no one has ever seen the bird feeding, that in Arbia it is sacred to the sun, and lives for 660 years; that when old age comes on, it builds a nest of twigs composed of cinnamon and thyme, fills it with scented herbs, and dies on it. From its bones and marrow there springs a creature like a little worm; from it comes a fowl. This animal, as its first act, performs the funeral rites to the former, and then takes away the whole nest to near Panchaja, a City of the Sun, and there places it on the altar." Lactantius Firmianus is worth quoting on this point—

Ipsa sibi proles, suus est pater et suus hæres,
Nutrix ipsa sui, semper alumna sibi.
Ipsa quidem, sed non eadem, quia et ipsa, nec ipsa est,
Æternam vitam mortis adepta bono.

Again, we have the words of Ovid—

Una est quæ reparet, seque ipsa reseminet ales ;
Assyrii Phænica vocant——

A better view of the matter can be obtained, as well as one of a more detailed nature, from the letter of Clement, of Rome, to the Corinthians, which Patricius Junius, its first editor, considered of the highest value. The words are as follow, and are taken from the revised edition of *Boeclerus* (in Programmat. Acad. xii., p. 61) :—" When, however, it perceives its own end approaching, it makes a small nest for itself with thyme and myrrh and other spices, and when its time has fully come, it steps into it and dies. Then, when the flesh has disappeared into a putrifying mass, a worm is born, which is sustained by the moisture of the defunct animal and begins to grow feathers, and having become stronger, it takes the nest where the bones of its parent are and carries them into Egypt, into the city called Heliopolis. There, in full daylight, and in the sight of all, it places them on the altar of the sun, etc." These words are almost identical with those found in Ovid (Bk. xv., Metam. Fab. 37), and stated with sufficient prolixity in Lactantius, who, among other remarks, has the following :—

Quæ postquam vitæ jam mille peregerit annos,
Dirigit in Syriam celeres longæva volatus.
Tum legit ærio sublimem vertice palmam,
Flagrat et ambustum solvitur in cinerem.

XIII. On this point, of course, many doubts are raised as to the precise nature of the material from which the Phœnix is said to spring. Ulysses Aldrovandus, in his very excellent work on Ornithology (Bk. xii., cap. 28), says :—" Pliny maintains that a creature like a very small worm is first of all created from the bones and marrow of the old Phœnix, from which there next springs a fowl." Philostratus, as quoted by Volaterranus, without any mention either of bones or marrow, has the nonsensical story that from the Phœnix, without any ashes, there springs a worm ; from the worm a new bird is born, which flies into Egypt from an unknown quarter. Suidas, though he gives us no authority, seems to follow this account. Tzezes, however, quotes the book of Philostratus in another light, when he maintains that this worm which has sprung from the ashes of the dead Phœnix is the parent of the new Phœnix. Oppian does not even mention this worm, but thinks that from the ashes alone there springs a fowl. It is from this source, again, that Orus Apollo gets his very different account of the birth of the Phœnix, when he says :—" Desiring to be born from the blood that flows from its parent's wound, which is inflicted by a violent though voluntary dashing of itself to the ground." So much for Aldrovandus.

XIV. We must now make a few remarks as regards the home of this imaginary bird. Pliny, Solinus, and with them Div. Ambrosius (Bk. v., Hexaem., c. 23), write that the Phœnix dwells in Arabia. Cornelius Tacitus and Athenæus tell us that it was first seen in the Egyptian city of Heliopolis. Nicephorus (Bk. xv. *Ecclesiastical History*) declares that it is found near the equator to the east and south. Claudian and Lactantius are quite opposed in view, and dream of some Elysian field or other, or of some kind of Utopian Paradise. Meanwhile, let us hear what Lactantius has to say :—

Non huc ex angues morbi, non ægra senectus
Non mors crudelis, non metus asper adit.
Luctus acerbus abest, et egestas obsita pannis,
Et curae insomnes et violenta fames.
Non ibi tempestas, nec vis furit horrida venti,
Nec gelido terram vere pruinæ tegit.
Hic genus arboreum procero stipite surgens
Non lapsura solo mitia poma gerit,
Hoc nemus hos lucos avis incolit unica, Phœnix,
Unica, sed vivit, morte refecta sua.

As to what food it eats, some maintain that it lives on ambrosia and nectar; others, on a very nourishing kind of dew. Ovid says its tears are of incense and its blood of balsam, etc. Of its note, which is the most tuneful and inimitable in the world, the greatest nonsense is talked; I am too annoyed to add anything on this subject; nay, my gorge rises at such falsehoods.

XV. Notwithstanding the flimsy nature of these facts, innumerable people have lived who have both accepted and promulgated them as historical truth. Of Ovid, Claudian, Virgil, and other poets I shall say nothing, for we must remember,

——Pictoribus atque Poetis
Quodlibet audendi semper fuit æqua potestas.

Tacitus, Solinus, and Philostratus are usually quoted from among the historians. The latter indeed is quoted by Conrad Gener, a Swiss Professor of Medicine and Philosophy now deceased (Bk. iii., p. 692, *De Avibus*), to the following effect :—"I believe the Phœnix is a bird which every five hundredth year flies over India on its way to Egypt." Can. Valerian tells us in Pliny that the Phœnix had flown over into Egypt. Sebastian Munster quotes a letter of an Ethiopian monarch to the Roman Pontiff. The following are its contents :—" In my country there is a bird called the Phœnix, the years of whose life are 300. This creature near the end of its life flies upwards so near the sun that it is burnt to ashes by the heat. Many of the fathers of the early Church, as for instance Ambrosius, Lactantius, Lyra, Tertullian, and, as Franzius declares, Nicephorus, allowed themselves to be imposed on by these nonsensical stories. Herodotus and Pliny went far more cautiously to work than these men. Would that they had done so oftener!

XVI. At this point we would have had to deplore the mistake made by Scaliger when he writes (Exerc. 133). "We read in the records of navigators, that the Phœnix is not absolutely a mythical creature. They affirm it is found in the inland parts of India. It is called the Semenda by the inhabitants." We are spared this task, however, by the fact that he seems in the following passages to abandon his faith in this story. Among recent writers Patricius Junius, swayed by the letter of Clement, has pronounced the tales

ANCIENT SCIENCE. 41

of the Phœnix to possess historical accuracy. Whether, however, this letter be fictitious, as some maintain, and as Boeclerus remarks, or genuine, the moderate judgment of Gerhard Joh. Vossius which is contained in his Christian Physiology (Bk. iii. cap. 99), is worth quoting. "It is not necessary to believe that Clement knew everything that might affect the secrets of nature."

CHAPTER II.

CONTENTS.

1. The Phœnix never seen except in pictures. Evidence of the Scriptures against the facts adduced in regard to it.
2. Nature herself does not admit such a flying creature. Reasons given.
3. A description of the Salamander. It does not live in fire. The reason.
4. The mythical story of the Phœnix upsets the peace of a healthy mind.
5. The source of these absurd stories.
6. The evidence of Laurenberg quoted and approved.
7. Is the Phœnix to be used, and if so how, to give point to a proverb, or to any other sayings of a similar nature.

I. This [fabulous] creature is quite a myth, and has never been seen except in pictures (I use the words of Herodotus). No man has ever seen it in true reality. Except a "'tis said," "'tis reported," "'tis a tale," or "so they say," no one can bring forward a clear statement in regard to the matter. (Gesner, page 692.) I regard as impossible, absurd, and openly ridiculous whatever, except in the way of a fiction, has been told of this creature. Such a belief as that in the Phœnix is a slander against Holy Writ, nature, and sound reason. We shall proceed regularly, and prove all our steps. Now, it is clear from the Scriptures that the Creator made male and female in all the brute tribes. With this intention the task of procreation was committed to all. To all alike did the same command proceed— "Increase and multiply." The Phœnix cannot be exempted from this command. And at the flood, not only did the quadrupeds but all the winged tribes go in with Noah, two by two of the unclean, and seven couples of the clean. The Phœnix is to be referred to the clean, nay to the most clean, class of animals, if any is. But where can we now discover either a male, a female, or seven couples?

II. Nature herself supplies us with arguments to defeat the defenders of the Phœnix. From death she declares there is no natural regress to life. The Phœnix, once dead, has entered on a stage of total extinction. This is the fiat of death. Nature declares that whatever is born into the world is born from what is similar to itself. In this work an equivocal birth has no place. If from a worm there springs a Phœnix, its birth would be doubtful, nay, the bird *itself* would be under a cloud of grave doubt. Nature says: "Birds are born from eggs, not from ashes." Birds likewise are oviparous, not viviparous. From the ashes of a fowl no one looks for a fowl, nor from those of a pheasant do we expect a pheasant. The same thing applies to the Phœnix. Nature tells us that without the fecundation and parturition of the female, no kind of creature can be preserved on the earth. Nature, too, teaches that no animal can be born from fire, nay, nor even be preserved in such great heat as is spoken of in the story of the Phœnix.

III. The statement made about the Salamander, to the effect that it can remain in the midst of flame without receiving any harm, is false. There is, however, as we intend briefly to show, such a poisonous creature as the Salamander, which is very like a lizard, and is very frequently found in Italy, of a black and tawny colour. Its tail is long and flexible, its skin rough, and it is marked with darkish spots on its back like stars. The statements of Galen and Dioscoris are more reliable. They say that the Salamander lives a long time in the fire, but is burnt and consumed by a too great heat. If fire can subdue iron, why should it not destroy a living body, which is soft and extremely porous? Though it may extinguish flame, it does not do this by the coldness of its body, but by its toughness, as is the case with many other kinds of flesh. The Salamander, however, succumbs to this. We may compare Scaliger, Exerc. 185. Now to return to our present subject.

IV. The Phœnix introduces the thinking mind to many and inexplicable difficulties. We shall relate some of the absurd stories. It is said that death is its life. When it dies it arises, and when dissolving away it is born again. Such nonsense! This bird is said to be of no sex. Our common sense tells us this is false. It is declared to be a solitary creature, and the only specimen of its kind. Sober philosophy demands that this doctrine be relegated to the regions of the absurd. Lucretius rightly argues:—

> Hûc accedit uti in summâ, res nulla sit una
> Unica quæ gignatur et unica solaque crescat.

There is an absurd story, too, that the Phœnix, by flying very high towards the sky, is scorched and burnt to death by the sun. The statement, in the first place, rests on a false supposition that the sun is the source of heat, and itself "warm" as they say. In the next place, so far is it from being the case that the highest region of the air is the warmest, those who have climbed the highest mountains in Italy, Greece, and the Canaries have always found the cold to be more intense. It is only the part of a madman to think that this bird lives so many thousands of years, as the world itself has neither been established nor shall be in existence so long, and at the same time to talk such an amount of nonsense about its death. All men must see the propriety of the words of the learned Laurenbergius, which are to be found in *The Philologer's Casket*, cent. ii., hist. 17.

V. In the meanwhile we shall make it a special point to speak freely what we think on those passages which relate to a matter which is obscure and covered with the veil of enigma. Next to the Hebrews, the Egyptians were the first to make use of and discover the liberal arts and sciences, as they were the first to employ various figures, paintings, and hieroglyphics. They were all kept secret, and lest they might come to be known among the common people, every effort was made to keep them hid. That age which we call $ἄδηλον$, that is uncertain and obscure, was a long one. The age that followed next we may consider the mythic or fabulous. In this, Poetry, especially that of Greece, and through her that of Rome, produced wide-spread traditions. We can the more freely pardon this art the crime of creating these fables, the more we remember the license poetry is allowed in whatever she touches. This is the source of the Phœnix story. It was by it as by a hierooglyphic that the ancients wished to indicate nothing more

or less than the constitution of this mundane machine, and the end of everything sublunary. We have the words of Laurembergius who, to the passage quoted above, adds the following:—
" I believe it has never been a real bird ; there is a secret meaning hidden under this fable. Namely, this bird called the Phœnix is a token of the whole world ; the golden head indicates the heaven with its stars, the bright body the earth, the blue breast and tail, the water and air. The Phœnix or world, however, will exist so long as the heaven and stars stand at that place where they were at the creation. When that ends the Phœnix will be dead, and if the old world renews its course everything will begin again."

VII. Such being the case, we consider that more caution and moderation should be observed in speaking of the Phœnix, in adducing evidence on the subject, in comparing similar statements made on it. For what is commoner than the saying, " A man with more lives than the Phœnix?" "A candid friend is rarer than the Phœnix," "To rise again like the Phœnix," " The Phœnix of literature." There used to be many men, and perhaps there are some still, who applied the words which are in every one's mouth in speaking of this creature, not only to martyrs and those who had died a death of piety, but to the Saviour and the resurrection of the dead.

My authority for this is B. Franzius (*Natural History*, part ii., chap. 3, p. 350). Cyprian (as Franzius tells us, p. 349) used the simile of the Phœnix to describe that mysterious divine birth which Christ taught. There is no doubt, however, that the holy father was speaking in a purely human sense. They have the best regard for themselves who, in any disputations, and only after permission has been asked or limitation made, use such words as these—" If what is told about the Phœnix is true," " If there be such a thing as the Phœnix, a matter which we do not enter into here," etc. To our mind the Phœnix is a pure figment and nonentity. Long ago this was the belief of such great men as Herodotus, Pliny, Gesner, Aldrovandus, Franzius, and Sperlingius. To God alone be glory!

Four Zoological Addenda.

I. Moles are not without eyes of their own. They have organs of vision, which have not been given them by nature without a use. They perceive men not only by the wind blowing the scent to their nostrils, but also by their eyes, which, however, are of the very smallest kind. Thus the proverb, "Blinder than a mole," is quite false. We may compare the recent dissertation on the " Power of Vision of Moles " by Thomas.

II. Dormice, although very much addicted to sleep, do not certainly live by sleep, and without any kind of food during a whole winter. Besides other reasons, we have the evidence of experience against such a supposition. They have been caught in the depth of winter in the very act of stealing eggs and chickens. Martial's dormouse is therefore mistaken when it says—

> Tota mihi dormitur hyems et pinguior illo
> Tempore sum, quo me, nil nisi somnus alit.

III. She-bears do not complete the work of gestation by licking the fœtus.

It is one thing to lick off the filth from anything; it is quite another to complete the process of gestation by licking. Scaliger says:—"In our Alps hunters have found pregnant she-bears, which, when cut open, have revealed the fœtus fully developed within them." (Exerc. 6.15).

IV. The hare species is not a totally hermaphrodite one.

To proceed from the malformation of certain individuals to assert the fact of a whole species would be the height of folly. Bodinus has the words—"These creatures are some of them hermaphrodite, but by no means all of them. This I have learned from an experienced hunter, on asking him to resolve a doubt I had on the subject."

On the Behemoth,

BY

GEORGE CASPARD KIRCHMAYER.

INTRODUCTION.

NATURE attracts us by a love of herself. She invites us to help her. Here by her diversity, there by her economy, here by her sublimity, there by her mirth, and anon by her world-wide gifts does the beautiful and ample mother of all display herself. We must therefore follow her in all we do. Although indeed sometimes and in some places she clothes herself in most beautiful garb, yet I am inclined to think that nowhere does this beauty attract us more than in the great tribe of the animal creation. It is not my intention to enter into disputed or doubtful points. We have all that we require at hand. We surely cannot get a better subject of consideration than the noble pair of huge animals called the Behemoth and Leviathan. The names of these creatures are familiar to all of us. May their nature be made familiar to the learned by the help of God's grace.

On the Behemoth.
1691.

CHAPTER I.

CONTENTS.

1. Passage concerning the Behemoth quoted.
2. In this passage, neither demon nor dragon, nor bull can rightly be understood as the meaning.
3. Narratives and confutation of the Rabbis.
4. By the Behemoth is to be understood the Elephant.
5. Etymology.
6. Different meanings of the word.
7. Synonyms of the term. The nature of oxen of Luca.
8. The uncultivated state of the ancient Romans. Varro quoted.
9. The elephant is next to man in the animal creation.
10. The intelligence of the Elephant.
11. His food.
12. His wonderful strength.
13. The configuration of his several parts. The Indian elephant can bend its legs.
14. Its natural armour.
15. Its meat and native country.
16. Its drink.
17. The method of capturing it.

I. That we owe the history of the Behemoth and Leviathan to Job, the most elegant writer on physics in sacred literature, and (with the exception of Adam, Jacob and Solomon, the wisest of all mankind) clearly the greatest authority on natural history, is proved by his 40th and 41st chapters. We get our knowledge of the Behemoth from the first, of the Leviathan from the second of these chapters. "Behold" says he, who is at once the Creator and Preserver of nature, "Behold now Behemoth, which I made with thee: he eateth grass as an ox. Lo now his strength is in his loins, and his force is in the navel of his belly. He moveth his tail like a cedar: the sinews of his stones are wrapped together. His bones are as strong pieces of brass, his bones are like bars of iron. He is the chief of the ways of God: he that made him can make his sword to approach unto him. Surely the mountains bring him forth food, where all the beasts of the field play. He lieth under the shady trees in the covert of the reed and fens. The shady trees cover him with their shadow: the willows of the brook compass him about. Behold he drinketh up a river, and hasteth not: he trusteth that he can draw Jordan into his mouth. He taketh it with his eyes; his nose pierceth through snares." So much for the words of the sacred book on this animal.

II. It is our duty to discover to what creature these attributes are to be assigned, and what is to be understood by the Behemoth. It requires very little insight to see that a creature of more than ordinary strength and size is here talked of. Those who, by rejecting all literal interpretation, seek an allegorical meaning when there is none, at once by one huge leap pass from natural things, and say that the devil himself is meant. This is the view adopted by Thomas and Lyranus. (See Dn. D. Olearius Conc. 49, *in Job*, page 388). Those who wish to see a comparison between the Behemoth and the devil drawn out can consult when they wish, Dn. D. Scultetus Conc. 232, *on Job*, page 310. For the present we shall pass over the attempt of Johannes Camerenses, who tries to transform for us the Behemoth into a dragon. Nor can we place much confidence in the idea of Sanctius,* who understands by the Behemoth a huge bull. The learned John Eusebius of Nuremberg, formerly Professor of Physiology in the Royal Academy of Madrid, takes much the same view when he says (Bk. xi. *Nat. Hist.*, chap. iii., p. 141), and maintains by every possible argument that an ox is meant in the passage quoted above.

---

* This Francis Sanchez, or Sanctius must not be confounded with the celebrated author of *De Matrimonio*. Francis Sanchez spent most of his life at Las Brocas, in Spain, and was a famous philologist, if the term can be applied to the pedantic grammarians of the 15th century. He died in 1600.

III. We shall, however, be much less ready to admit the silly stories of the Rabbis. Rabbi Abraham declares that the creature is a monstrous and unnameable animal. Rabbi Moses, that the word *Behemoth* is a sort of collective for all the ox tribe. By a similar disregard of what the real meaning is, one could vindicate the myths of all the writers on the Talmud. The circumcised Jews maintain in sober earnest, that it is a huge ox whose head is one mile, its neck one mile, and its body seven miles long. They say this beast feeds over a thousand mountains each day in Paradise, until Messiah comes and slays it as a pleasant dish for the Jewish people. See a lengthy account of this by Buxtorf, (in Synagog. Jud., chap. 36., p. 466.) Compare Gerson (Thalmud p. 94 cap. 46).

IV. We now bring forward our own view, and maintain that that creature is meant by the Behemoth to which alone all these passages can refer, if their meaning be not distorted. The Elephant alone can be meant by the word Behemoth. This assumption of ours we have now to prove. We shall proceed bit by bit, and shall fix the name as belonging to the Elephant alone, and show that the facts stated can only be applied to it.

V. The Elephant gets the name of Behemoth, which is a feminine and plural noun, just as if we were to call it "cattle." The Hebrew phrase in this passage denotes excellence, and "Behemoth" is applied to the Elephant because, by reason of its enormous bodily size, it can overcome many beasts. It denotes the highest wisdom. (Proverbs i. chap., v. 20, and ix. chap., v. 1.) By similar reasoning the Elephant is called θηρία by the Greeks, as we are told by Suidas. I have also seen several passages quoted from Latin authors by Ulysses Aldrovandus (Bk. i., chap. 9, p. 97, on Quadrupeds). The Latin word is itself derived from the Greek word meaning a hill or small mountain, as Isidorus shows. Such a thought must have been in the mind of Oppian, unless I am mistaken, when he wrote—

Ut si illum videas dum immania corpora versat,
Excelsi montis procera cacumina credas.

By others the word ἐλέφας or ἐλέβας is derived from the participle βὰς of the verb βαίνω and the noun ἕλος, which means a marsh, because it is a well-known fact that the male and female Elephant are in the habit of copulating in marshes.

VI. We have now to clear away some ambiguity attaching to the word, and that in a few sentences. Pliny speaks of the Sea Elephant, and says it is so named from the exceeding brightness of its tusks and its great size, in which respect it resembles the land elephant. (Pliny, Bk. ix., chap. 5). I believe that in this passage he is referring to the walrus. There is, besides, a kind of locust which rejoices in the name of Elephant. Let us quote a passage from Pliny (Bk. xxxii., chap. 2). "The locust which goes by the name of Elephant is black, and has four cloven feet; it has, besides, two arms, with two joints, and one toothed claw on each." There is also a kind of jug which goes by the name of "elephant," as we read in Athenæus (Bk. ii., chap. 5).* Elsewhere, in the same author (cap. 16), Epicinus says:—

" . . . hodiè ad Clepsydram
torrentis instar aurigabor utraque,
est autem elephas. Elephantos attrahit rhytum,
quod congios capit duos . . ."

VII. We must also touch on the different names for the Behemoth, and that in a few words. By the Latins it is called *pecus Indicum*, and especially "*Bellua Lybica*" Some call it *barrus*, whence we derive "*barritus*," the cry of the elephant.† Horace asks—

" Quid tibi vis mulier nigris dignissima barris?"

By Lucretius elephants are called "snake-handed bulls." His words are—

" Inde boves Lucas, turrito corpore tauros
Anguimanos belli docuerunt vulnera Pœni
Sufferre."

---

* "Idoneum nisi tibi elephantum puer ferat. Quid est hoc per Deos? Poculum magnum, choarum quod trium sit capax," etc.

† And hence, also *barritone*.

He has wisely given them this name, for it is a fact that the Elephant uses his trunk like a hand. He bends it back and forward, contracts and stretches it. It can be twisted about because of its flexibility, can be moved with great ease, and can be wound round like a serpent. The most common of the other names of the elephant is the Luca cow. The reason of this is as follows :— Pyrrhus, King of Epirus, when summoned by the inhabitants of Tarentum against the Roman power, first opposed the Romans with herds of elephants in Lucania, where they had never been seen before. By consulting Pliny, we find from Book viii. of his *Natural History*, chapter 6, that elephants were first seen in the war with King Pyrrhus in Italy, and were called Luca cows, because they were seen in Lucania.

VIII. We know that the Romans of old cultivated their own farms and were their own ploughmen. And what is strange, asks the learned Rupert (p. 259), in their giving animals the names they did? They called the ostrich the "great sparrow," the camelopard "the wild sheep," panthers "African mice," lions "Numidian bears," and they were led to this, like country folk and children, by making a comparison between these new animals and those which they knew as native in their own country. Virgundus shows this (Super Flor., Bk. i., cap. 18). Lipsius had denied, on the authority of Pliny, that there were any bears in Africa Salmasius opposes Pliny and Lipsius with the authority and evidence of Herodotus, Strabo, Virgil, Juvenal, Martial, Solinus, and Marcus Antonius Sabellicus. We are now ready to return to the subject of the Luca cows. M. Varro laughs at the derivation we have given above, and rebuts the opinion of those who think that the elephant was called the Luca cow or Luca bull from the word Lucania, declaring that it is not in accordance with the Roman turn of mind. "I believe," he says, "that they got the name of Luca cows from the word lux (light), because of the far-shining glitter produced by the towers placed on their backs, which were ornamented with gold shields."

IX. Having done with the word itself, we now pass on to the matter in hand. We have made the Elephant the subject on which we are to speak. We shall, in order, apply to it the attributes we quoted from Job. "Behold now Behemoth which I made with thee; he eateth grass as an ox." This squares exactly with the Elephant, which was created with man on the sixth day of creation to live on the earth. Nay more, this creature, contrary to and beyond the nature of wild animals, loves man and delights in his society. He allows himself to be led hither and thither by a timid Arabian boy, and suffers himself to be beaten by him. Pliny very truly says (Bk. viii., cap. 1), "The Elephant is the largest of animals, and comes nearest to man in instinct. It has been taught by its intelligence" (I would prefer to call it its power of using its instinct), "obedience to man's tongue and its master's orders, and remembers favours received; nay more (a rare circumstance in man), it can be guided by goodness, prudence, and justice." These are the words of Pliny. But he stupidly makes a further remark in the same place, to the effect that the keeping of faith, the worship of the sun and moon, and some silly prayers or other, are accustomed to be paid to the Creator by the Elephant. Pliny is here advancing from the actual to the imaginary. Ælian (Bk, v., c. 49) incurs similar censure. Lipsius is much more cautious in his praises of the Elephant. He says—"I make no doubt that there are many true statements made concerning this animal, but there are also many which overstep the truth. Is there anything so strong as to bear whatever weight is put on it?"

X. The statements however of the well known Vertomannus on the wonderful similarity between the elephant and man, are not displeasing if received by a healthy mind. He declares that "he saw certain elephants which appeared to him to have more sense than the men in some districts." A man is always a man, and a brute a brute. Yet man weighed down by natural stupidity, or sunk in barbarism, or otherwise degraded, has little if any of the divine in him, (I am excepting his reason which sometimes he is unable to use) to distinguish him from this most intelligent creature. This at least is true that none of all the brute creation approaches nearer man than the elephant. The elephant accordingly takes the palm of superiority before the lion. He has a more noble nature. "At Rome not long ago, (I quote from Aldrovandus) several elephants were taught wonderful tricks, and to perform evolutions very difficult to explain. One of their number, less tractable than the rest, and the recipient accordingly of more frequent scoldings and blows, was surprised during the night practising and teaching himself of his own accord." We have ourselves a very few years ago seen this creature taken through many states and cities of Germany, a perfect marvel of intelligence. It leaped in time to music, threw a javelin, waved a flag, looked for a coin that had been hidden, and, by means of its trunk, found it and returned it. In short it did everything in the most prompt manner at the nod of its keeper.

XI. The Elephant is said to eat grass like the ox. It is well known it is not a carnivorous creature like the lion, eagle or vulture. Nor is it a devourer of insects like the nightingale, lapwing or swallow. Nor is it omnivorous like the magpie, crow or raven. Cardanus (Bk. x. Subtil.) has the words "It must needs live on shrubs, fruits and grasses, for otherwise it could not possibly be a good animal. For we know that all animals which live on flesh are savage, cunning cruel and pugnacious." Aloysius Cadamustus, quoted by Ulysses Aldrovandus (Bk. i. de quadrup. p. 214), bears witness to the fact that they feed most eagerly on the leaves, and even the very trunks of trees. Diodorus Siculus, following the Sacred Scriptures, says that they frequent mountain pastures and reedy fens. When their ordinary food fails them, they do not scruple to eat roots, and certain fruits such as melons, apples, and barley. At Onold, I saw eight huge loaves devoured by an elephant in a short time. Nor does it disdain wine. Custom is here a second nature.

XII. The strength of the Elephant is tremendous. They carry towers filled with armed men against the enemy, and with a sword tied on to their trunk, fight with great effect, committing great havoc amongst the men upon whom their keeper urges them. Cardanus says "They have such bodily strength that two of them can pull upon shore a laden vessel of the largest size." The Indians have a habit which they still keep up of fastening two iron chains round the elephants belly, and fastening by this means a wooden saddle on its back, on which is placed a small tower, in which seven men can stand upright at a time, (sometimes even as many as fourteen) all armed for battle. But why need we delay over minor details? An elegant passage occurs in Maccabees vi., v. 37¹, where it is stated that each Elephant carries a tower, and in each tower there are thirty-two men, not counting the African driver. Ælian is our authority for stating that elephants were formerly used to pull down the walls of an enemy's town. With their trunk alone they can toss up full armed men. Ctesias himself saw an elephant uprooting a palm with its tusks at the command of its driver, and pounding it beneath his feet. One should get a sight of two of the tusks of this animal, and not laugh, when he is told on the authority of Cardanus, ' Bk. x., p. 319, that Vertomannus saw a pair that weighed 325 pounds. Julius Cæsar Scaliger himself saw a single elephant's tooth (whence we get our ivory) longer than a man (Exerc. 204, sec. 1). "I have seen," he says, "a tusk far taller than myself." Those which come from India are found to be the larger and stronger.

XIII. We now pass on to a consideration of certain parts of the elephant. In this connection we must use the moderate language of Job—"He moveth his tail like a cedar; the sinews of his genitals are wrapped together. His bones are as strong pieces of brass, his bones are like bars of iron." The testicles of the elephant are here the first point of consideration. The male elephant's organ of generation is not very large. Cardanus says that it reaches to the ground, although this is denied by some. We shall pass over this point, and consider the colossal size of its bones and its feet. Its legs are rough like columns, and make deep footmarks on the ground. Its thigh bones go down straight, and do not bend outwards like those of cattle. Hence it is, that the joints of its knees are so level with its legs, that unless one saw its legs bending one would say there were no joints at all. Hence, also, has arisen the idea that the elephant has no knee-joints, so that if it once falls on the ground it cannot rise again. With this remark it was that Diodorus Siculus and Strabo persuaded many men of the truth of a false account of the capture of elephants in the woods. The elephants lean, they said, on the trees which form their usual sleeping-place, but which in the meanwhile have been almost completely sawn through. I have seen these animals lying down and at once rising up again at the word of their owner. Others have done so too, and the fact is beyond all doubt.

XIV. We have now to give a description of its superiority to other animals, and of its natural powers of defence against attacks. The paths of God are glorious. The Elephant is the first of the works of God, for among quadrupeds it is the highest and the chief work of God next to man. Again, the elephant is said to have been created first of all living quadrupeds. My authority for this is Dn. D. Olearius (Conc. 49, Job, page 388.) However that may be, we maintain that next to man the first place is to be given to the Elephant in preference to the lion. Our reasons for this we have already stated. The nearer anything comes to man, the more exalted is it to be reckoned. We have already pointed out the extremely docile nature of the Elephant. To our own words those of Pliny may be worth adding (Bk. viii., cap. 3). " Mutianus, who was thrice Consul, is my authority for saying that one of these animals learnt the formation of Greek letters." Ælian says :—" I have seen with my own eyes an Elephant writing Roman characters on a table with its trunk quite correctly, and without any twisting. Nay more, while it was writing, its eyes were steadily fixed on the table, so that one would say that it was keeping its attention fixed and following what it wrote." Nothing of such a nature can be said about the lion. It is a solitary creature. The Elephant delights in a royal retinue. The lion is a cruel beast: the elephant docile beyond belief. Clemency becomes a king. The lordly Elephant rejoices in its armour. " He," says Job, " that made him can make his sword to approach unto him." We must remember it has gleaming tusks besides its trunk, which it uses as a sword. Aldrovandus well says—" It uses its trunk like a hand, and can so handle everything with the point thereof, and so use it for grasping objects, that not even the smallest coins can escape it. It even takes them up and hands them with its trunk to the keeper who is seated on its back." When about to cross a river or a deep lake it breathes through its trunk, which it keeps raised aloft, thus affording a remarkable instance of the prudence and foresight of nature. Pliny says—"They eat with their mouth, but breathe and drink and smell with what has not inaptly been called their hand." (Bk. viii., chap. 20.)

XV. "Surely the mountains bring him forth food, where all the beasts of the field play. He lieth under the shady trees, in the covert of the reed and fens. The shady trees cover him with their shadow; the willows of the brook compass him about." We have already spoken of its food in the paragraphs preceding. Here now we have a description of the Behemoth from the point of view of its quietness and habits. The Elephant is docile by nature, and can be tamed at the first attempt. Oppian is worth quoting.

Illi vastus inest animus, dum saltibus errat,
Et ferus ; est homines inter mansuetus et æquus.

Herbiferis etenim atque umbrosis vallibus olim
Fagos atque oleas et celsa cacumine palmæ,
Sæpe solo stravit, firma sub radice revulsa,
Ingenti incumbens et acuto robore dentis;
Ast ubi in humanis manibus versatur eundem
Deserit ille animus, fugiuntque immania corda,
Namque jugum patitur, durisque stat ora lupatis,
Et pueros tergo discit gestare magistros.

Thus, although the Elephant is a strongly-armed creature, it is yet contented with grass, and it kindly removes with its trunk from its path those animals that walk in safety round it, to prevent their being hurt by any unforeseen motion of its own. (Dn. D. Scultetus, p. 316.) When they have eaten their fill, they return to their moist and marshy retreats and seek the reedy pools, there to lie down. At other times they never enter the water unless compelled, although their great delight is in it. They have the greatest difficulty in their attempts at swimming, on account of the very great size of their bodies.

XVI. "Behold he drinketh up a river and hasteth not; he trusteth that he can draw up Jordan into his mouth." Drinking is with the Elephant a slow and very long process, and it takes up such a large supply of water at once that one would think it meant to imbibe the whole river. It does not, however, drink till it has put its feet into the water and disturbed it. Camels and horses have the same habit. It is wonderful how the brutes know what is best for themselves. Pure water is said to produce colic in their insides. Aristotle says—" The Elephant takes at one meal nine Macedonian measures of food, and generally drinks six or seven." This huge supply is required by the huge size of its body, and is not the consequence of the mere pleasure of eating. This Sperlingus rightly maintains in his Lectures on Zoology (chapter on the Elephant, p. 5).

XVII. "He taketh it with his eyes; his nose pierceth through snares." Some take this sentence as absolute, others understand it as put interrogatively. We have no wish to disparage any one's opinion on the subject. Our authority for the view we have taken is Diodorus Siculus and Pliny. The Elephant, although the largest of the animal creation, has yet natural enemies. Its greatest dread is fire, and the next pigs, the grunting of which it cannot endure. But its greatest enemy is the serpent. This creature, seeing the Elephant drinking beside the river, or feeding leisurely, suddenly springs at its eyes, and sometimes gouges them out, sometimes with the coils of its long tail takes such a grasp of its trunk, that it is either strangled as by a noose, or prevented from defending itself. Thus the serpent sucks its blood, until the Elephant is either overcome by exhaustion, or, deprived of sight, dies outright. See Diodorus Siculus, Bk. iii., chap. 3; and compare Pliny, who has precisely the same account, Bk. viii., chap. 12; and Solinus, chap. 38. On the ordinary and multifarious methods of hunting the Elephant our chief authority is Aldrovandus, and next to him B. Franzius, in his *History of Animals*. We have been compelled to enter thus into detail about the Elephant, which is not a whit less than we should have required to prove that any smaller animal was meant by Job. It is a fact that by no other animal can all these attributes be justly claimed.

END OF VOL. II.

Printed by E. & G. Goldsmid, Edinburgh.

[COLLECTANEA ADAMANTÆA.—XV.]

Un=Natural History,

OR

MYTHS

OF

ANCIENT SCIENCE;

Being a Collection of Curious Tracts on the
Basilisk, Unicorn, Phœnix, Behemoth or
Leviathan, Dragon, Giant Spider,
Tarantula, Chameleons, Satyr,
Homines Caudati,
&c.,

NOW FIRST TRANSLATED FROM
THE LATIN,

AND

Edited, with Notes and Illustrations.

BY

EDMUND GOLDSMID, F.R.H.S.,
F.S.A. (Scot.)

IN FOUR VOLUMES.

VOL. III.

PRIVATELY PRINTED
EDINBURGH.
1886.

[COLLECTANEA ADAMANTÆA.]

Myths of Ancient Science.

*This edition is limited to 275 small-paper copies,
and 75 large-paper copies.*

COLLECTANEA ADAMANTÆA.—XVI

Un=Natural History,

OR

MYTHS

OF

ANCIENT SCIENCE;

Being a Collection of Curious Tracts on the
Basilisk, Unicorn, Phœnix, Behemoth or
Leviathan, Dragon, Giant Spider,
Tarantula, Chameleons, Satyrs,
Homines Caudati,
&c.

NOW FIRST TRANSLATED FROM THE LATIN,

AND

Edited, with Notes and Illustrations.

BY

EDMUND GOLDSMID, F.R.H.S.,
F.S.A. (Scot.)

IN FOUR VOLUMES.

VOL. III.

PRIVATELY PRINTED.
EDINBURGH.
1886.

The Leviathan.

CHAPTER I.

ARGUMENT.

1. A quotation.
2. The Crocodile not really meant here, nor the Serpent, nor any of the monstrosities of the Rabbis.
3. By the Leviathan is meant the Whale.
4. Incredible size of the Whale. A collection of instances.
5. The huge rib of one preserved in the Church of Wittemberg.
6. The extremely dangerous character of the capture of the Whale.
7. The same continued. The Indian method of capture.
8. The sinking of ships by the Whale. Its pranks in the sea.
9. Conclusion.

I. We have now to pass from the largest of land animals to the largest of those that live in the water. The name of this beast is the Leviathan. The Hebrew root of this word is "Lavah" which means, assumption, accretion, accumulation, increase. Hence Leviathan, whose size is remarkable. (Franzius, *Animal Histor.*, p. 604). The Latins call it the Cetus.

There are very many kinds of the Cetus. The chief is the common whale, next to which come the Orca, the Physter, the Dolphin, the Scolopender, and the Sea-cow. We are quite assured that in the present instance reference is made to the common whale because of the attributes claimed for it. The words of God in the 41st chapter of Job should be familiar to us: "Canst thou draw out the Leviathan with an hook? or his tongue with a cord which thou lettest down? Canst thou put an hook into his nose? or bore his jaw through with a thorn? Will he make many supplications unto thee? Will he speak soft words unto thee? Will he make a covenant with thee? Wilt thou take him for a servant for ever? wilt thou play with him as with a bird? or wilt thou bind him for thy maidens? shall thy companions make a banquet of him? shall they part him among the merchants? canst thou fill his skin with barbed irons? or his head with fish spears? Lay thine hand upon him. Remember the battle, do no more. Behold the hope of him is in vain! shall not one be cast down even at the very sight of him? None is so fierce that dare stir him up."

II. We cannot in the present place give any attention to Beza who understood by the Leviathan, a Crocodile or some kind of aquatic serpent. We must at the same time exclude certain pervertors of the text who maintain that nothing but a serpent is here meant. The notion of R. Kimchus we must also dispense with, to whom the word Leviathan signifies some kind of very large serpent destructive to ships. I cannot listen for even a moment to Rabbi Manasseh Ben Israel, when he prates on the Resurrection of the Dead, (Bk. ii., chap. 19, p. 225), and says that by the Leviathan is meant that banquet which God shall prepare for those who have lived good and holy lives on this earth. Rabbi Moses Majemon has a similar fiction (in More Nebuchim, part iii., chap. 23, p. 404), where he says that under the Leviathan is included all the general properties of all bodies, which are dispersed among all the animals that fly swiftly, or walk. In the Talmud, the ridiculous idea of a fish three miles long has been introduced as the daily food of the Leviathan. (Compare Buxtorf. *In Synagog. Iud.*)

III. We, however, will dismiss these silly tales, and continue our argument. That only is properly meant by the Leviathan which, without any figure of speech, can claim all those qualities attributed it. We cannot, even if we wish, make the Leviathan larger by any efforts of our own. When put to the test, it is found to be less than supposed. We have first, however, to make some remarks on this vast and unconquerable sea-monster. Everything tends to the conclusion that the claims we make for it are right. No animal in any sea approaches in size, terribleness, and ferocity to the Whale. None surpass it. I shall prove this (1), From its great size, (2) from the extreme difficulty of its capture, (3) from its extreme ferocity, (4) from the impossibility of all intercourse between it and man, (5) from the extreme difficulty of killing it. These points can be proved from the description we have given of it above.

IV. That fish must surely be of vast size which could swallow the prophet Jonah with one gape of its jaws, and throw him up again after three days unharmed. There was a Whale taken in 1531 at Harlem, in Batavia, which was of the ordinary kind, 68 feet long. In 1577, not far from Antwerp, there was another taken in the river Sheldt 85 feet in length. The one which was captured in 1532, having been cast up on the shore by the waves, was of immense size. A part of it appeared out of the water, a part remained buried in the waves. Though greatly mangled and destroyed by the ravages of beasts and fishes, yet so much of it remained as to be beyond the capacity of one hundred huge waggons to remove. It was 30 cubits in length. The gape of its jaws embraced a space of 6½ cubits. Its jaws were 7½ cubits in length. It had 30 ribs, each of which was 21 feet long. The length of its head, from the base to the snout, was 8 cubits : its tongue was 7 cubits in length. But we must be brief. The reader may find several other particulars of this fish in *Letter to Polydore Virgil*, which can be seen in Franzius, part iii. (*Animal Hist.*, chap. 2.) The same writer has also the following account :—" In 1545, in Pomerania, at Gryphiswald, there was taken a small Whale, in which there was yet found an immense amount of fishes not yet digested, and among the rest a living salmon, three feet in length. These fishes filled three casks. Hieronymus Welschius (chap. v., on Italy, p. 33, which see) will be found to give an account of Whales of a size more remarkable than any yet seen.

V. While on this point, it may not be out of place to mention the very large rib of a whale which is preserved in the chapel at the Castle of Wittemberg. This rib is 14 feet long, and was deposited in its present place (where it is fastened to the wall by an iron chain) by the late Elector of Saxony, Frederick the Wise. It can be seen by visitors, and there is a label attached on which the following verses are inscribed, according to the spirit of that age :—

> Omnes interrigenæ prægrandem cernite cete,
> Bis septem pedum, costa de latere tensâ.
> Cunctipotentis opus, non perscrutabile cuivis,
> Perspicuis undis sub, talia monstra creavit.

VI. Many accounts are given of the method of capturing the Whale. All these accounts are extremely diffuse, though this is a circumstance scarcely to be wondered at. Oppian, Albertus, Rondeletius, and Ulysses Aldrovandus, who took his materials from these writers, should all be consulted. (Icthyol., Bk. i., on Whales, page 261). We shall deal with the matter, which is a tedious one, in as short a manner as possible. Twisted ropes are taken about the thickness of a cable, to which is attached an iron chain, furnished with a very strong and sharp hook. On this hook a piece of ox meat is placed for a bait. The braver part of the men row up to the place selected. The Whale, as soon as it scents the bait or sees it, makes for it with haste and avidity, and, unsuspicious of treachery, takes in the whole hook. This causes a serious wound, and it at once attempts to get rid of the iron chain to which the hook is attached. After a long ineffectual effort to do so, and goaded to madness by the excruciating pain caused to its vitals by the constant pulling back and forward of the hook firmly imbedded within it, it plunges to the bottom. Then the hunters slacken the rope, which is furnished with air-bladders at various intervals.

VII. The Whale, having plunged to the bottom, remains quiet for some time, but the bladders keep the creature, though wishing to rest, from doing so, because the air in them tries to come to the surface. The Whale now rouses its anger, and pursues the bladders with the intention of punishing them, and under the impression they are the creatures that are causing it pain. The bladders, dragged along by the ropes from above, flee before it. The Whale, as is its custom, sinks again to the bottom. The bladders sink after it. The creature, which has drawn the bladders after it, is in great pain, and gets in such a terrible fury, that, lashing the waves around it, one would think Eolus himself was lodged beneath. The Whale, after a long and weary struggle, and with its strength now almost gone, is compelled to follow the rowers who pull the rope in the nearest boat. Then at a given signal the hunters approach it with their boats, and amidst mutual cheering and encouragement, with great courage and in the midst of loud shouting, as if they were in the middle of a battle, they proceed to attack the animal. The Whale is now surrounded on all sides by the hunters armed with javelins, harpoons, prongs, scythes, axes, knives, and spears. The Whale endures the blows showered upon it undisturbed, and spouts forth great masses of water from its blow hole. The hunters endeavour to drive it towards shore, piercing it with constant wounds, and not without danger to their own lives. The merchants and their comrades help them to close up its blow holes, and last of all to kill it outright when it is divided amongst them. The East Indians indeed have a different method of taking it, and one attended with greater risk, and requiring greater courage for its accomplishment. They leap on the creature unawares, and ride on its back, and then by piercing it deeply with bamboos, they close up the air-holes and thus despatch it. An extremely clear account is given by Gothofredus. (Part i., page 13, *History of West Indies.*)

VIII. We can see from the above account, the meaning of Job's words in speaking of the Leviathan. They denote the extreme difficulty and not the impossibility of capturing and killing the Whale. Surely the Whale can with the greatest difficulty be brought alive into the possession of man. Its ferocity is indomitable, its strength incredible. None dare attack it in the open sea. It sinks whole ships without any difficulty. It is a remarkable fact that ships newly painted have a great attraction for whales by reason of their smell. The creatures come up to a vessel and rub themselves against it. The sailors, somewhat in fear for the safety of their vessel, throw out painted barrels to induce the Whales to leave the ship, and the Whales play and sport with them. The Batavians, English, and the Danes take the Whales annually on the coasts of Greenland and

Iceland, and that, too, in considerable quantities. The Indian Ocean is said to breed the largest size of Whales. The writers on such subjects tell us that Whales have often been seen whose eyes and eyelids were like a soldier's head with a large helmet on it. Again, Rondeletius, quoted by Sperlingius, has the words—"I have seen the penis of a Whale of such a size that, when moved by a powerful man, it yet reached the ground on either side of him. From this one can get an idea how huge it must be when the Whale is roused by desire." This gives us also a clue for measuring the rest of the body. The mighty Creator herein glorifies his own majesty, first by the example of the Elephant, and then by that of the Behemoth. "Who then," he says, "can resist my countenance?"

IX. Let this suffice for the Whale. We need not describe it more minutely, for the same reasons, and for others, that we refrained from going into detail about the Elephant. Nor, again, need we enter further into the subject of the method of generation, tenacity of life (which, from the evidence of zoologists, seems in the case of both to extend to 300 years), or several other points connected with them. Our position is, that by the Behemoth is meant the Elephant, and by the Leviathan the Whale. We have rested our proof on the principles and doctrines of natural history. We are so far, however, from turning aside from any one who has a better theory to propose, that we shall reverence him the more. The works of God are manifest, and always to be magnified. Can there be as much power and majesty in the irrational creature as there is in the Creator Himself? He has thrown a veil over his divinity in all things, nor has He left Himself anywhere without a witness. 'Tis ours to admire, to search, to obey, and to adore.

On the Dragon,

BY

GEORGE CASPARD KIRCHMAYER.

PREFACE.

ON the sixteenth of October of this year,* news was brought from Rome of a Flying Serpent that had been killed by a hunter after a severe and dangerous struggle. This story, which appeared more like some fable than real truth, was a subject of discussion among the learned. The circumstance was denied by many, believed by others, and left in doubt by several. We have heard the opinions of men on this subject, even though it be itself a mythical one. May their memory be allowed to rest in peace, and their great names be undisturbed. Day unto day showeth knowledge. We owe also a debt of gratitude to those who have investigated the subject according to the best of their powers. Nature will be our model, truth our quest: God our helper.

* 1691.

The Dragon.

CHAPTER I.

The Nature of (Serpents) Dragons.

CONTENTS.

1. Various etymologies of the word Dragon.
2. Different things to which the name may be given.
3. The same continued.
4. Synonyms of the word.
5. Definition of the Dragon. Its antipathy to man.
6. Passages of Ælian examined.
7. Different views brought forward. Size of the Dragon.
8. Examples.
9. Great Strength of the Dragon.
10. Antipathy to the Elephant. Numerous instances thereof.
11. The native country of the Dragon.
12. The Dragon is the king among Serpents.
13. Its poisonous nature. It has no breasts.

I. The derivation of a word is far from being an unworthy subject of investigation, as we are frequently told. Becmannus,* following Ambrosius

---

* Christian Becman, a forgotten Theologian, who died in 1648.

Calepinus,† derives the word Dragon from "derkein," that is, "to see," or look. The reason of this is, that the Dragon is an extremely quick-sighted creature. Hence it is represented in the poets as guarding treasures and prisons. Another explanation of this derivation is that it is very watchful and wakeful, like other cold-blooded creatures. To the Dragon it is, I believe, that Ovid addresses the verse—

Terrigenesque feras, insopitumque Draconem.

Jul. Cæs. Scaliger gives a somewhat different account—namely, that it is derived from "dran," to do, and "achos," pain, because it is a poisonous and deadly creature. His words are—"Grammarians and good authorities have derived the word Dragon from "derkesthai." My opinion is that it should rather be taken from "dran" and "achos." It is of little consequence to our present subject which of these two accounts is taken as the right one. Perhaps it is not an error to go to a Hebrew source for the derivation of this word. In this language "darak" means he has " walked or gone ;" hence comes " darek,"a "way" or "path." Thus not only do the letters agree exactly with their original, but the thing signified corresponds

---

† Ambrosius Calepinus was the author of the celebrated Dictionary that is indissolubly connected with his name. He died in 1510.

exactly with the term. These creatures move by creeping, and by a series of small leaps. The Dragon is the largest of the Serpent tribe.

II. The term itself (to pass on to its different meanings) is usually applied not only to men and brutes, but also to plants and to a certain mountain. Draco was that well-known ancient, stern legislator of Athens, who wrote his laws not in ink, but in blood. (We take this statement from Demas' *Apud Dul. Gellium*, bk. xviii., chap. 12, *N. H.*, and from Scaliger, *Exerc.* 112.) That these laws were, however, abrogated by Solon on account of their excessive severity is well known to every scholar. There was also a certain Dracus, leader of the Achæans, who was conquered by Lucius Mumius, a Roman general, as Livy tells us (in his *Epitomies*, bk. lii.). The greatest, however, of this name is the famous Sir Francis Drake, of Plymouth, who last century sailed round the world to its very limits. A man at that time second to none in naval glory, he was learned in the laws, pursuits, customs, habits, and other remarkable points of many peoples. There is a sea fish which is commonly included among the animal creation under the name of "the dragon." Without reference to Scaliger, we cannot determine whether this creature differs from the Sea Spider mentioned by Pliny, bk. ix., chap. 48. We know, indeed, that Scaliger calls this the true

Dragon as distinguished from the false. The following are his words:—

III. The creature is called the Dragon, not from its shape, but from its hurtful nature. It is a long and thin animal, while the true Sea Dragon is quite different. There is a dried specimen in France of this shape, and without feet, but furnished with bat's wings. Its head is serrated, and its crest comes to a peak on its head. It has a flexible tail, two feet in length, and bristling with prickles. The skin is like that of a skate." We also meet with a "Dragon" among the catalogue of plants. Old vine-shoots which have borne the brunt of many years are called 'Dragons' from their knotted appearance. See Pliny, bk. XVII., chap. 22., *Nat. Hist.*, and compare Scaliger Exerc. 169., page 2. I shall not now speak of the dracunculus. We have now to refer to the mountain which bears the name of Dragon. We shall be brief. It is situated in Asia near Imolus. Imolus lies in Cadmus. Pliny should be consulted, bk. V., chap. 29. These meanings are, however, all foreign to the present discussion. Our present purpose is to speak of the Serpent of this name, and to describe it. We shall now proceed to this.

IV. The different names of the Dragon are as follows:—In Hebrew "tanin" means a Dragon, but it also means a Whale. Derivation of the Greek

"Drakon." We have to notice how the Greek termination "on" becomes "o" in Latin. It is quite a usual change. Thus Leon becomes leo; Dion, Dio; Lacon, Laco. The Dragon is called the King of Serpents, as the Regulus is the King of the smaller kinds of Serpents. That the Dragon should be called a Winged Serpent is neither a new fact nor a remarkable one. I shall give a reason for it further on. It is known to some as the "ringed" and "large" Serpent. Franzius answers a questioner on the subject with the words:—"The Dragon is nothing else than a Serpent with coils of a marked nature and swollen by some means or other. Hence arises the common saying—"Unless one Serpent swallows another, you cannot have a Dragon." By the French it is called Dragon, by the Italians, Dracone. By ourselves through a rare agreement of pronunciation it is called 𝔇𝔢𝔯 𝔇𝔯𝔞𝔠𝔥𝔢.

V. We have now to proceed to the main matter under discussion. The Dragon is without doubt a Serpent of the largest size, of terrible strength, fond of waste places, the King of the Serpent tribe, and especially marked by the strength of its tail. There is nothing surprising in the fact that a medley of purely accidental qualities should be chosen to distinguish this creature when very little is known of its shape. It belongs to the genus of Serpents, and is a reptile of warm blood, cunning, poisonous, and a deadly enemy of man. The original antipathy between man and the devil has even extended to the natural Serpent. Although B. Franzius quotes examples from Ælian and other writers of a certain sympathy between man and the Dragon, yet this cannot be taken as evidence for every day experience. The Dragon is no more a friend of the man who happens to protect it against its destroyers than are the lion, eagle and wolf, animals which in rapacity and cruelty are certainly second to none. Many things are said in favour of the tribe, but the case is thus misunderstood. The Devil himself frequently lurks under the form of a serpent to deceive man. Deep-seated in our mind, there remains the remembrance of the great deception that old and wicked Dragon the Devil wrought in our first parents. Let him who wishes find love in his heart for the Dragon. I neither give it nor take from it any feeling of such a kind.

VI. I am not ignorant indeed of what Ælian says of the infant Arcas and the Dragon. My answer is a short one. There have been mixed up with the truth, several mythical details. I think one might as well put faith in what the same zoologist tells us elsewhere, (viz : bk. VIII., chap. 9., Aleva) about the Dragon that fell in love with a girl in Idumæa. Here Ælian gives us a flowery little sentence. He says—"Animals are therefore not devoid of reason." Yet even though it be granted that Dragons have fallen in love with beautiful boys or girls, I maintain that they did not act thus by reason of a desire for man or for his beauty. They pretended to be his friends, not for his, but for their own profit. Ælian himself (bk. viii., chap. 9) certainly says—"It is the nature of animals to love not only their own kind, but even others which may be beautiful." We have been somewhat prolix in the above statements because of the universal false tradition that has settled in credulous minds. Similar tales are common about lizards. But let the man who wishes to keep clear of harm, beware of those who practise deceit.

VII. We have begun with its size, for it has a vast body. In respect of size, it occupies exactly the same position among reptiles that the Elephant does among quadrupeds. The famous Alexander, whom we call the Great, on account of his great achievements, met with Serpents of great size, (viz: 16 cubits long) when on his great expedition to India against Porus. Ptolemy, King of Egypt, required an army of armed horsemen to attack a Dragon of great bulk, and 30 cubits in length, which after great risk to his own life, and after the death of some of his followers, he only managed to kill at last by stratagem. Diodorus Siculus, as quoted above, gives us a long account of this event, (bk. iii.) In India Dragons grow to such a size that they can swallow both stags and bulls, as Pliny tells us, bk. viii., *Nat. Hist.*, chap. 14.

VIII. In the same place he tells us how in the time of the Punic War, (*i.e.*, the Second Punic War, as we can gather from Livy, bk. xxx), beside the river Bagrada (which as Dalechampius tells us is now called the Megerada) a Prince of Attica went out at the head of his whole army and attacked, as it were a city, a Dragon 120 feet in length, nor did he stop until he had put it to death.

In the lives of the Kings of Poland, a story of King Cracus (who built Cracow) is often met with. There was a Dragon which lived in a rock, and which when compelled to do so by hunger, used to creep from its cave and kill many people. Three oxen were daily brought to the cave of this monster. The King of the country moved with compassion for his people, ordered at last a calf's skin to be filled with pitch, sulphur, and nitre, and offered to the beast. The Dragon was deceived by this trick, and with one bellow from its vitals perished on the spot. Compare Florus Polonicus, John Pastorius, bk. i., chap. 3. Those who care for further information, should consult Ælius lxv., c. 21., and especially M. Paul Venet. bk. ii., chap. 40., p. 381. *History of Tartary*

IX. We shall now proceed to the second characteristic of the Dragon. This is its terrible strength. This fact is proved by its vast stature, its insatiable voracity, the difficulty of capturing it, and the symmetry of its limbs. On the former points we have already spoken; on the last we have something yet to say. Another Dragon, with which Alexander the Great had a fight in the arena, was 70 cubits long when only part of it was seen, and had eyes, as Ælian states, as big as a large round Macedonian shield. M. Paul Venetus has seen Dragons larger than this in Caraiam, a province of Tartary. It is no wonder that these creatures fight with the Elephant itself. By winding their coils round their legs, they squeeze them so tightly that the huge beasts cannot move. Then by raising their necks under the trunk of the Elephant they strike their fangs into its eyes, and, blinding its vision by their fiery and lightning-like glitter (I use the words of Diodorus Siculus), they dash it to the ground, and then tear it to pieces.

X. They are the sworn foes of the Elephant, and there is nothing so large, so wild, so powerful, or active which they will not at any moment fight either as an equal or as an inferior.

The antipathies in Nature are remarkable. Thus there is enmity between the lion and the scorpion. The poison of the weasel is instant death to the Basilisk, the most poisonous of all Serpents. The gadfly is the crocodile's enemy. The ichneumon hates the asp with all a stepmother's hatred. The newt is the deadly enemy of the scorpion. Mice and cats are sworn foes. Cats and dogs are seldom found to agree. The chameleon and snake, the stag and hawk, wage constant war. The cock flies before the kite, the sheep is the victim of the wolf, the hare that of all.

It must, however, be noticed here that we are far from believing that every single Dragon attains to the same point in respect of size or strength. The individual varies with the locality, with age, and with other circumstances. It has never been gainsayed but that the largest Dragons are found in India.

XI. A third point in our description of the Dragon was its native haunts. It is an inhabitant of desert places. It loves marshes, secluded and inhospitable spots. Hence it is called especially the inhabitant of the desert. Malachi i., 3. In the sacred writings God is described as going to make a lasting devastation. "It shall be a habitation of Dragons and a court for the daughters of the owl. The wild beast of the desert shall also meet with the wild beast of the island, and the satyr shall call to his fellows." The same horrible desolation of Dragons is foretold in Isaiah, chap. xiii., v.

22. Compare Job. xxx., v. 29. Hence, also, they are commonly found in untrodden forests and caves. "The young of the Dragon (says Franzius) feel extreme thirst in the middle of summer, and where they are unable to get water, their cries, like those of the ostriches, are terrible to hear." Yet they are said to be commonly found in Lybia, Egypt, Arabia, Æthiopia, and India; that is, in countries well known to be very warm in climate.

XII. Further, our description of the Dragon included the right of dominion (so to speak) which it wields over other reptiles. Thus, from its incontrovertible supremacy, writers have given it the name of "king." Although the basilisk must not be cheated out of its name and dignity, yet it must only be taken into consideration when speaking of the smaller reptiles. The Dragon is the largest, bravest, most powerful, and most formidable of all reptiles. These are all royal prerogatives. Last of all, our description of the Dragon included an account of its natural armour. For its strength lies in its tail, and it can use it to such good effect that elephants of great bulk fall before it. In the same way the elephant itself fights with its trunk, the lion with its claws, the horse with its hoof, the ox with its horns, the boar with its flashing tusk, and the wolf with its teeth. No power can avail to release anything once folded within the embrace of its enveloping coils.

If small snakes and small or ordinary Serpents can break a man's arm, what must we think of the power of the Dragon?

XIII. Is the Dragon equally powerful by reason of its poison? This has been a question among scholars, and a negative answer has been given by many. Pliny has denied (though wrongly) all poisonous qualities to the Dragon, saying, "The Dragon has no poison." But seeing that it is a Serpent, and that experience gives evidence of a contrary nature, we can put no trust in Pliny on this point, for the Dragon does poison the air. Some have attributed breasts to the Dragon from an erroneous interpretation of *Threnius*, chap. iv., vers. 3. It is not the Dragon, but an animal of higher rank, that is here meant, as Franzius clearly shows, and he is followed by Sperlingius. The evidence of our own eyes also infallibly proves it.

CHAPTER II.

On the Varieties of the Dragon, and chiefly on Flying Dragons.

CONTENTS.

1. The Variety of Dragons.
2. Dragons are admitted to be both winged and flying. Cardan noted.

3. A recent piece of evidence from Rome proves this. A monster taken in Ireland last month.
4. Evidence of Matthew Merian, Breuning, and of Benzo, as to Dragons with wings.
5. Confirming evidence of Paræus, Scaliger, Nierembergius.
6. D. Thom. Bartholinus following Franzius takes the same position as we do.
7. Does the Dragon then belong to the bird species. No. Reasons given. The bat is no bird.
8. Flying-fish are also admitted to exist. Evidence for this.
9. Conclusion.

I. We do not wish to give a decisive opinion either one way or the other, as to whether the Dragon is a distinct species, or merely a variety of a genus. Distinguishing characteristics can neither be derived from the places wherein it is found, nor its size, nor even from the variety of its colour. English and German dogs, however much they may differ from one another in magnitude and in locality, are yet one and the same species. Such a distinction as that implied in the present subject, could only be brought about by a very distinct configuration of certain parts of their bodies. Some, says D. Franzius, are furnished with feet and wings, some not. Some are red, others black, others of an ashy colour. Some are 5 cubits long, others are 10, others 30, others 40. Johannes Eusebius Nierembergius says:—"It can coil itself up into a high coil, and thus contract its size, as Philippus Pigafeta tells us in his description of the Congo. There is there found a two-footed animal of the size of an egg, and with the shape of a Dragon. It is winged, and has a long tail. Its head is also long, and its mouth is furnished with several rows of very sharp teeth.

II. There are, therefore, some Dragons with and some without wings. In saying that there are winged and flying Dragons, we know we have to meet the scepticism of Cardanus, and the downright opposition of others, who on other points are considered amongst the most circumspect of modern writers. These men maintain that flying and winged Dragons must be brought under the head of the mythical. But even the well-known incident reported from Rome has appeared to very many ridiculous and absurd. I quote Cardanus:—"I saw," he says, "at Paris five two-footed creatures with very small wings, which one could scarcely deem capable of flight, with a small head, with a head like a Serpent, of of a bright colour, and without any feathers o hair. The size of the largest of the five was about that of a small rabbit." The opinion of Prof. Daniel Lagus is worth quoting—"We must not, from the weakness and small size of these little Dragons, rush precipitately to a conclusion regarding the whole species." We shall not at present quote any further authorities.

III. The story that comes from Rome has

given us an opportunity of doubting previous ideas on this subject. The spectators of the fact have vouched for the certainty of the story. On the 27th of October, 1660, the following circumstance was described as occurring at Rome:—A "winged Dragon appeared in the Campagna, which, after wounding a hunter, was killed. Yet the hunter himself eight days after (doubtless by the influence of the poison) expired, and his whole body became of a green hue." We shall not here trouble ourselves with the question whether the Dragon is a stranger to or an inhabitant of Italy. At the same time, I would be unwilling to believe that the creature flew by itself across from Africa or Asia over so many miles of country, and I should be the last to state it as a fact. For even in our own European countries some monstrous births occasionally take place. For instance, last month (on the 6th of November) at the Hague there was found a certain naked wood monster, a male completely covered over with hair, and which the poets used to call by the name of Satyr, who was surrounded by hunters and killed. What are we to make of this? We shall speak of this not now, but later.

IV. This is the point we have at present to demonstrate—that there are such things as flying and winged Serpents. I use the word winged in the sense of furnished with wings, although not with feathers. Let me quote some writers on this point. Matthew Merian, in his *History of the Antipodes*, part ii., page 211; next, the well-known and learned Eastern traveller, Joan Jacob Breuningus, chap. 26, says:—"I saw, among other things, a certain extremely tall and huge two-footed Serpent, furnished with a pair of wings like the bat." Hieronymus Benzo, in his account of the New World and of the French expedition to Florida, chap. 4, p. 480, says:—"I saw a certain kind of Serpent which was furnished with wings, and which was killed near a wood by some of our men. Its wings were so shaped that by moving them it could raise itself from the ground and fly along, but only at a very short distance from the earth." We have here occular proof: we should surely admit other proof after this.

V. Ambrose Paræus, formerly chief counsellor to the King of France and a doctor of Paris, in the first book of his *Studies in Surgery*, page 51, quotes from Pliny that Dragons were found in Ethiopia of the length of 10 cubits. "But," he adds, "in India there are bird creatures of 100 feet in length, which fly to such a height that they pounce on their prey from the middle of the clouds." Evidence on this point is to be found in Scaliger also, Exerc. 183, sect. 5. The words are—"The mountain range which divides the kingdom of Narsinga from Malabria is the haunt of many wild beasts. Among these are winged snakes, which hide among the trees. These are said to kill those who come too near them by a single hiss, or even by a look." (This is surely an exaggeration.) John Eusebius Nierembergius, a leading naturalist, agrees with us in our view of the subject. See the 12th book of his *Natural History*, chapter 36, page 282.

VI. Franzius, again, was far from being of an opposite opinion to us when he wrote in the 4th part of his *History of Animals*, chapter 5, page 741, the words—" There are two kinds of true Dragons. Some are winged, with a kind of pinion made of membrane, and which have their wings not composed of feathers, but of membrane fastened to the back instead of ordinary wings. The great Thomas Bartholinus, also, the son of a great father, in his Treatise, published at Pavia (chap. 7, p. 50), on the Unicorn, has painted in vivid colours, and with faithfulness to the original, a flying Dragon in the museum of Tobias Aldinus. The skeleton of this creature Louis XIII., King of France, gave as a present to Cardinal Francis Barberinus some years before.

VII. Nor let any one object that whatever flies is a bird. It would not be sufficient evidence for the matter in hand. What are we to say to the bat? It is a flying creature, but it is no bird; notwithstanding any restrictions

Franzius may put upon his admission of the fact. We can easily adduce proof if required. It is not an oviparous, but a viviparous animal. Now, birds lay eggs. It is not furnished with feathers, but rather with wings and hairs. Nay, it has also got breasts, and likewise suckles its young. Again, it has teeth; it has long ears and pointed teeth. It squeaks like other mice. I quite deny, therefore, the validity of the argument of those who place the bat among birds. In this way we should be compelled to include the flying fishes for the same reason among the birds—a very absurd idea.

VIII. There are, without doubt, such things as flying fishes. I shall not speak of Scaliger, where he criticises Cardanus in the words—" You write you have seen the dead bodies of flying fish : I have seen them alive. In the Gulf of Venice, between Venice and Ravenna, and more than two miles beyond Quioza, in the year 1550, a flying fish was caught, as Ambrosius Paræus tells us." (*Studies in Surgery*, bk. xxiv., p. 736.) Andrew Thevet, in his *History of the World*, writes that when he sailed across to the New World, hundreds of flying fish, called by the inhabitants of the forests Bulambech, were met with. These creatures leapt up from the sea and passed over 50 yards in their flight, and by frequently striking on the sails or mast became food for the sailors.

A confirmation of the same statement is to be found in the *History of Brazil*, by John Lerius. The Normans, under Duke Nicolas Durence Villagogne, a Knight of Malta, captured an innumerable quantity of flying fish. See a detailed account of this fact in the *History of the Antipodes*, by John Lewis Gottfried, to be found in Matthew Merian, p. 318, in his *History of the West Indies*.

IX. Does any one think of giving these fish the name of birds because they fly, forsooth? In fact, just as the mere possession of the power of flying does not argue conclusively for the creature possessing it being a bird, so also the absence of it does not prevent the creature in question from being one. Thus the ostrich, though devoid of neither wings nor feathers, cannot fly; but all the same it is a bird. Just as, again, because we cannot deny the power of swimming to the Dragon, are we to class it as a fish? Man, the dog, the diver, the frog, pumice stone, and apples, have all the power of floating. There are, besides, insects, worms, caterpillars, bugs, and so forth, which have the power of floating. A subject is to be studied and determined, not by properties which it has in common with others, but by those which are peculiar to itself, and not by some only, but by all. We here conclude our remarks about the Dragon.

On the Spider,

BY

GEORGE CASPARD KIRCHMAYER.

PREFACE.

THE Spider is a wonderful architect. It is to this clever little creature and its flimsy threads that we owe our idea of subtlety. The scholarly Scaliger, *Exerc.* i., sect. i., *On Subtlety*, says:—" It would seem that we have derived the word from the idea of fine threads, which in a finely spun web escape the quickness of the eye. Hence a part of the signification has been taken and applied to other things." We look up to geometers; we wonder at rope walkers; we admire weavers, whether men or women. These things are all very well. But we never think of looking at the Spider, because it is an every-day occurrence, and can be seen by every one. Thus everything, though endowed with admirable qualities, if only it is common, at once falls in our estimation. Thus the greater number of scholars there are, the less do we think of them. Solomon, in the far past, was struck with admiration of the Spider, and even in the present day we admire and watch it. It is a born geometrician, rope walker, and weaver : not a made one. It is wise without a teacher, shrewd without a guide, skilful without a master. Its subtle powers must be investigated, and may God help our endeavours.

The Spider.

The Spider. A Particular Investigation.

CONTENTS.

1. The Spider praised by various writers.
2. The etymology of the word.
3. A double meaning of it explained.
4. Continuation of the same.
5. Synonyms of the word.
6. The nature of the Spider. The distinction drawn between perfect and imperfect animals rejected.
7. The shape of certain of its parts.
8. The Spider very poisonous. To the fowl, however, it is harmless.
9. Its foresight and cunning, as quoted from Pliny.
10. Seneca's judgment praised. The claim made by some for knowledge on the part of brutes and the conception of finite purposes denied.
11. Various proofs of this.
12. The method of generation of the Spider, as shown by Aldrovandus.
13. Difference of opinion as to the composition of the material formed by this creature.
14. Democritus defended. Aldrovandus criticised.
15. Proof given.
16. Its home, food, time of spinning, age, and antipathy to other creatures.

I. This is the little creature on whom Nazianzenus has bestowed higher praise than he has on

Euclid. Aristotle, in treating of the skill of insects, after saying that he considers the race of ants and bees before and excelling all animals in industry, adds that the Spider is the more skilled in the business of its life. This conclusion is come to both from the fact of their workmanship in weaving their webs and from that of their industry in working and hunting. The great Magnus Aldrovandus believes that it could only have been from the Spider that weavers, linen-weavers, and tapestry-workers learnt their arts, whether we regard the perfection of their fabric or the symmetry and indissoluble combinations of their complete web. The words of Claudian Ælianus on this point are learned and well chosen (*Hist. Anim.*, bk. vi., chap. 57). We shall first consider the term, and then the subect it involves.

II. The terms "araneus" and "aranea" are quite interchangeable, though Suidas does not agree with us on this point. Greek furnishes us with the immediate origin of the word. The term " arachnes," or " arachne," is the same in Greek as "aranea" in Latin. We thus see that the "ch" has been dropped and " a " added. Although, like Aldrovandus, many wish " arachne " to be derived from its having its " ichne," or foot-marks, very indistinct, or from its taking away these footmarks into the " aer " or air, yet we shall, without disparaging any, give another derivation of the word. "Arachne" surely comes from the Hebrew, meaning "it has woven," or "it has spun." Indeed, is the name of a Lydian girl, daughter of Idmon, who, as Pliny tells us, was the first inventor of linen and network. This Arachne, if we are to follow the stories of the poets, did contend with Pallas for the palm of good workmanship. She is said to have lost, and to have been turned into a Spider by the victorious goddess. And it is thus, they say, that "aranea" is derived from "arachne." Ovid is worth consulting on this point. (*Trans.*, bk. vi., fables 1 and 2.)

III. Now, to keep clear of all danger that might arise from a doubtful acceptation of the word, we have to take note of some errors that have been made. For (1) there is a sea fish which is called the Spider. It has eight feet, very long in proportion to its body, which is small. This is the reason of its getting the name of Spider. This fish is itself, as Bellonius tells us, very common in every sea. Others refer it to the crab genus. By the Latins it is called the dacunculus, or sea dragon. By the French it is termed vive, because when caught it can, contrary to the nature of other fishes, live for a long time out of water. The English call it viver; the people of Marseiles areque. Pliny, bk. ix., chap. 48, and bk. xxxi., chap. 2, *Nat. Hist.*, should be consulted on this point. (2) The Aranea or Spider is an animal of the weasel or mouse kind, with a poisonous bite, which destroys anything that may cross its path, as Pliny holds, bk. viii., chap. 58. (3) The Aranea, again, is the woolly or hairy seed that grows on the willow. Pliny, bk. xxiv., chap. 9, *Nat. Hist.*, says, "The fruit of the willow before becoming ripe becomes woolly."

IV. Again (4) the term Aranea or Spider was formerly applied to a certain part of the astrolabe. Cælius, indeed, when treating of the gnomon and astrolabe and their parts, bk. xii., chap. 9., says:— "The third part is called the Dicptrice, containing in its sheath the membranes on which are drawn the equator and the tropics. Then over these membranes is drawn what is called the Aranea, in which is the zodiac, etc." (5) Again the term Aranea is even taken to mean a peculiar blight among olive trees. It is a kind of bug or some small worm, as I gather from Scaliger (*in Theophrastus* iii. ; *On the Disease of Plants*, chap. 20). We may consult and add the testimony of Pliny, bk. xvii., chap. 25., *Nat. Hist.* We must not however be too diffuse. Again (6), the word Aranea often means the web, or the effect, as well as the Spider, the cause. (7) Nor is it uncommon to use the term as applying to that meteoric phenomenon (called the threads of the blessed Mary) which commonly in spring and autumn moves in a circular path through the atmosphere. On the term arachne or aranea as denoting the proper name of a girl, though the fact was mentioned above, there is no need of more than ordinary attention. Neither of these meanings have any thing to do with our present subject. The former of these words however (Arachne) we shall treat of in the sixth paragraph.

V. Different names for the Aranea must now be given. By the Hebrews it is termed Yakarish, which stands for the creature as well as the web. By the Greeks it is called Arachnes, and Arachne indifferently, just as the Latins use Aranea and Araneus. Suidas, indeed, does draw the distinction that Arachnes is the animal and Arachne the web. But the truth is that this distinction as we have already said is worth nothing. Thus in Dioscoris we find the creature "Arachne;" and in Plutarch the works of the "Arachne." By the Germans it is called the spinner, from its spinning or rather *vice versâ*, the term spinning being derived from the spinner. For from its work the art of weaving (as Beckmann says in his "Origines" p. 338) took its beginning, just as the art of sewing did from the workmanship displayed in the leaves and bark of trees, or architecture from the empty caves of nature and the nests of birds; or as the art of flute-playing sprang from the sound of water, or the sigh of the trees. As Lucretius says:—

> Zephyri cava per calamorum sibila primum
> Agrestes docuere cavas inflare cicutas.

VI. To proceed, however, to the real subject of our discussion. In our opinion the Aranea is an eight-footed insect, poisonous, endowed with great foresight and cunning, and oviparous, and especially remarkable for the web which it weaves from out of its own body with wonderful industry. We have put it down as an insect. The reason for this is not far to seek. Insects, are small and weak animals. As is the case with the bee, the fly, the butterfly, the locust, the worm, and the ant, so it is with the spider. One cannot strictly refer insects to the flying, creeping, wading, or swimming classes. By the Greeks they are called entoma. That is either from the incisions and marks with which they are ornamented either on their back, belly, or on each side of their body. We cannot admit the distinction that has been drawn between perfect and imperfect animals, nor can we say to which of the two classes the Aranea belongs. Insects have all that is necessary for them to have. This is the case with the bee and the ant, and is true of the Aranea as well. If they had other additional qualities they would no longer be the bee, ant, or Aranea, but something else. "God beheld everything that he had made, and behold it was all very good." Now, what is good is perfect. Conceive goodness, and then call it imperfect in its essence. You will have badness, not goodness. Suppose a distinction is drawn between absolute and relative perfection, and we enquire into the meaning of the former term. We should lose ourselves altogether. An enquiry into the meaning of the latter idea results in a contradiction. Thus several things would have to be called imperfect which are not so.

VII. Seeing the Spider is eight-footed, it exactly corresponds to the crab. The feet themselves vary in length, according to the various uses they are put to. Some of their feet they use to thin out and lengthen the threads they spin (I quote from Ulysses Aldrovandus, bk. v., *On Insects*, chap. 13, p. 241); others are employed to turn these threads into the web and join them together; with others, again, they run along these threads, and hang motionless from them when they like. Their front and hind legs are the longer, the middle ones the shorter. With the hind feet they arrange their threads and join them in the woof with inimitable skill. Their front ones they use as hands, and seize the prey that falls into the webs; their middle limbs are used to help them in this. Thus do we learn that

God has given nothing to the world without its use.

VIII. But secondly. We described the Spider from the point of view of its being a poisonous creature. The remarks of the late Sperlingius help us at this point (chap. 6, *On Insects*):—"The poison of the Spider when taken by man, whether in eating or drinking, gives great and terrible suffering. The patient is troubled sometimes with fever, sometimes with stiffness, sometimes with itching, and sometimes with swellings. Spiders are eaten without danger by cocks and other birds. Thus, though poisonous to some, it is not so to all." There are many herbs poisonous to us, such as the napellus and hemlock, which are harmless to brutes. Pigs delight in the stinking excrement of other animals. Such possesses neither any useful nor attractive qualities for us. Several kinds of small birds feed on various worms, while we eat these birds without harm. Thus what is a pest to one is not so to all. Men often die in heaps when the brutes are untouched, and again the latter perish when the former remain unharmed. Again, the Spider does not inject its poison by striking, like the scorpion, but by its jaw, or bite. Hence as soon as they capture a fly they fetter its legs and bite it, and, as the poets say, breath a poisonous breath on it, and last of all kill it outright, after they have sucked every drop of blood from its body.

IX. Again (thirdly), our description of the Spider included its faculty of foresight and cunning in the subtle work of weaving its web. The ant, indeed, is a foreseeing and cunning creature, but it is far surpassed in these qualities by the Spider. The silkworm, though of wonderful industry and skill, is far surpassed by the Spider. The scholarly words of Pliny are striking (*Nat. Hist.*, bk. xi., chap. 24):—"With what delicate touch, with what fine thread and equal, does it construct the main supports of its web, using its own body as a counterpoise! It begins to weave from the middle, and works in a circle, joining together the cross threads. Leaving spaces at certain intervals, but gradually increasing from the middle, it fastens the whole with an indissoluble knot. With what wondrous art does it conceal the snares that lie in wait for its prey in the chequered nettings! How little, too, would it seem that there is any such trap laid in the compactness of its web and the tenacious texture of the woof, which would appear of itself to be finished and arranged by the exercise of the very highest art. How loose, too, is the body of the web as it yields to the blasts, and how readily does it catch all objects which come in its way. You would fancy that it had left the thrums of the upper portion of its web unfinished. With what architectural skill, too, is its web arched over, and how well defended by a nap of extra thickness to keep out the cold. How carefully, too, it retires into a corner and appears intent on anything, all the while that it is so carefully shut up from view that it is impossible to perceive whether there is anything within or not. And then, too, how extraordinary the strength of the web when the winds blow on it! When is the wind ever known to break it, or any accumulation of dust to weigh it down? The web often stretches between two trees when the creature is exercising its art and is learning to spin. The thread stretches from the top of the tree to the ground, and up this thread the Spider passes and repasses, and weaves at the same time the threads required. Then, when a victim has fallen into its power, how ready it is to run and seize it. Though it be caught in the extreme outside of the net, the Spider invariably runs to the middle, because by so doing, and by shaking the whole fabric, it most effectually entangles its victim. Then it repairs the rents made, with all a tailor's exactness."

X. Again the words of a wise Roman are most apposite. "Seest thou not what skill the bees have for making their own cells, what concord reigns among them for executing the work given them by a divine Providence? Seest thou not how inimitable is the web of the Spider? What a work it is to arrange the threads, some of them placed in straight lines as a foundation, others running round in a circle, and becoming fewer and fewer as the centre is left. Their object is to capture the small creatures as with a net." This happy phrase is worthy of immortality. "The Spider's art is inborn, he says, not learned;" for the young Spider as soon as hatched has a complete knowledge of the art of weaving a web, and begins the work. It has not seen, nor has it learned wisdom from former experiments. Without doubt these and other skilful animals possess their knowledge as a gift of nature. Following the interpretation of D. Freitag (*Disp. Anti. Sperling. de Orig. Form.*, th. 19), and of Dn. Leifold (*in Not. ad Jaceh. Phys.*, bk. ii., chap. 10, p. 171), Melchior Cornoeus '(*in Currie. Phil. Tract* 3 *dub.* 14), and John Tatinghov (chap. 8, p. 194), have argued that this is not the case, and maintain that these creatures neither have any thought nor are they endowed with any kind of natural wisdom.

XI. We shall not here enter into the question as to whether nature performs all the operations she does with a distinct end in view. And no end can be a motive or cause to work unless it is recognised as such ; nor can there be such a thing as a desire for an end which is unknown. But at the same time we do not intend to dwell at great length on the manner in which nature performs all her operations in the wise and regular way that she does ; nor on the question as to how the brutes themselves seek out, and accommodate means to ends ; nor again do we wish to quote the great names of Tycho Brahe, Armand de Bello Visu, Roderick de Arriaga, Thomas Fienus and others. Let us quote the words of Solomon :—"There be four things which be little on the earth, but they are exceeding wise. The ants are a people not strong, yet they prepare their meat in the summer : the conies are but a feeble folk, yet make they their houses in the rocks ; the locusts have no king, yet go they forth all of them by bands. The Spider (not the Stellio as the Vulgate renders the word), taketh hold with her hands, and is in king's palaces." Compare, as especially confirming our theory, the words of Nierembergius, bk. i., *Nat. Hist.*, chap. 18, p. 11.

XII. When talking of the Spider we said it was an oviparous creature. When the female has spun out and shaped its web, the male comes and helps it. When this process has been repeated several times, the process of copulation is gone through, turned in opposite directions. This is rendered necessary by reason of the globe shape of the stomach. The experiment of Aldrovandus deserves notice ; he says :—"After examining the eggs of the Spider, on one occasion I found them to be numerous, of a moderate size, darkish, covered with small spots divided, separated from one another, and sticky. If any are by any chance lost, the spider makes diligent search for them, and even carries them in its mouth. I have seen likewise from a single egg, innumerable fœtuses born, yet so small as scarcely to be discernible by the eye. Still as soon as hatched they wove threads so fine that nothing could be more marvellous. I have also noticed under the stomach of a Spider which I had caught, a large heap of eggs so small as to resemble atoms.'

XIII. The fifth characteristic of the Spider related to the material with which it spins its web. I maintain that it is from the internal viscous substance of its own body, and not from the outer covering of wool that the Spider spins its web. Aristotle denies this, and laughs at Democritus for maintaining such an idea. The philosopher of Abdera (Democritus) had held that the Spider weaves its web from the viscous substance of its stomach at certain very brief intervals of time. Pliny says:—"It begins its web, and the womb of the creature is sufficient for the material required either by some process of disintegration in its body at a stated time as Democritus says, or from some source which produces the wooly substance within it." Ælian opposes Aristotle, and says:—"The creature does not get its thread from any other source than its own stomach, it constructs its hunter's net for the capture of its minute quarry, and spreads it out in the shape of a pole. Then it replenishes its stomach with that substance which it has drained it of for constructing its web." The words also of Ovid long ago on the transmutation of the Arachne into a Spider are very fine.

XIV. It is remarkable that on a subject so clear, Aldrovandus should have committed such a mistake. "Justly," he says, "has Aristotle destroyed the idea of Democritus. For Spiders and other small creatures of the same kind take very little nourishment, and have very little to support their life, on account of the small quantity of blood and heat inside their bodies. Therefore seeing they do not eat so much food as would account for the consumption that goes on in the process of weaving their webs, we should be reduced to the conclusion that more comes out of their body in the shape of surplus matter and excrement than goes in, in the shape of food; a conclusion which is absurd." The statement given here is false, and no consequence flows from it. We shall afterwards refute and answer it. At present, howeverr, let us put Aldrovandus against himself. He denies of Spiders, but asserts elsewhere of silkworms, that they spin their silk threads from their own bodies. Yet the silkworm is an annulose creature, and seems only to consume enough food to account for the amount of silk it spins from its body. And a little further on he quotes Vida, an Italian poet—

————effundunt quaesita par aevum
Stamina, dites opes uteri.

XV. But behold when, after the vacation last autumn, I was trying some slight experiments on nature, and was hunting for Spiders of all sizes, I discovered, after repeated observation, that the material out of which they spin their threads is a dark, spotted, glutinous, and sticky humour, very similar to kneaded dough, and of a dark, sparkling hue. It is from this substance that they spin out their fine threads through the womb, which is situated beside the haunches. This process they perform while walking on. On the 7th of September, from a Spider which I had fastened up on a beam by means of a pin I drew out an unbroken thread 66 feet in length. And on the following day, from another Spider of medium size I took a thread, a very fine thread, which, though sometimes broken, was yet 170 feet long when stretched. On pricking the womb of the creature with a needle it was found still to have some of the rich viscous substance in it. Thus when the Spider was dead and cast aside, I have taken threads from it, though with very great difficulty. Any one who cares may try the experiment. The Spiders at least cannot be charged with ignorance of this art of spinning. Thus when caught (for they are silly creatures, and when caught in a chip of wood must be quickly thrown to the ground, frightened or kept prisoners in spittle) they suspend themselves and hold on by the thread which they spin like rope dancers.

XVI. There could have been here added some remarks on the native countries, food, usual time of weaving, age, and its occult antipathy to other animals, of the Spider. We give a few on the native country of this creature. There is no country which does not produce the Spider. Nevertheless, near the town of Gratianopolis (it is commonly called Grenoble), in that part of France next to Italy, Grandentius (bk. iv., c. 50, *Memorat.*) tells, as well as Merula in days gone by, that there is an old tower which is quite free from Spiders or any venomous reptile. Nay, further, they say that if any are brought into it they perish on the spot. We see from Aldrovandus, page 241, that the Spider is content with very little food. They feed on juicy and viscous substances, as can be seen both from *a priori* and *a posteriori* arguments, for they usually live by catching flies and bugs, from the bodies of which they extract their juicy blood. Besides, their womb is full of viscous humours. As regards the time at which they weave, we have the following remarks to make. They very seldom make their webs when the sky is clear, but only when it is overcast. Hence they foretell cloudy weather. There are also other signs to be drawn from this creature. For instance, they make their webs higher than usual when the rivers are to be in flood, as Pliny tells us. Crowds of flies and Spiders, a most unusual phenomenon, are an indication of pestilence. Our authority for this is Athanasius Kircher, in his recent tract on the *Plague*, page 144. Again, by their leaving a house they foretell it is going to fall.

The life of the Spider is a short and fragile span, for they soon reach their maturity, and what takes little time to create, takes little to die. Again the Spider is a friend to no other animal. The Germans have on this fact founded a proverb. Indeed they often fall upon and destroy their own kind. They are said to wage wonderful wars on the stellio as Aristotle says; again they have an irreconcilable hatred for the toad. See Laurentius (*Cent.* 5, *Hist.* 78, *Acerr. Phil.*) where he gives a wonderful incident that occurred to a British monk.

On the
Sting of the Tarantula,

BY

HERMANN GRÜBE.

On the Sting of the Tarantula,
And its Cure by Means of Music.

§ I. Symptoms Produced by the Sting of this Creature.

My object being to give an account of the Tarantula, or poisonous Spider of Apulia, so called from Tarentum, where large numbers of them are found, I shall not delay over a long revision of what has been long ago said by other writers, but shall treat of the sting of the creature and of the power of music in curing it, and shall be brief in proportion as others have been prolix. I shall thus have two heads under which to treat my subject, the first dealing with the sting of the Tarantula, and the symptoms arising from it, and the second giving a short account of the power of music to heal such stings. The first difficulty which one meets with is the number of symptoms of the poison, which, according to Scaliger, *Exercit.* lxxxv., *contra Cardanus*, is almost equal to that of the days of the week. Those who are stung by the Tarantula are, some of them, seized with laughter, others with weeping, others with continued wakefulness, others with stupor, others with nausea and vomiting. Others, again, have a cold perspiration, dizziness, or delirium. Some run about, others sit listless, and seem as if seized with lethargy. Some are affected one way, others another, and so diverse are the symptoms that some believe there are as many kinds of this animal as there are kinds of affections produced by it. Scaliger, however, dissents from such a view, and considers that such diversity of symptoms arises from a diversity of temperament among those who suffer from the stings, just as the different effects which are produced in people by the excessive use of wine or tobacco arise from the different constitutions of those who partake of these stimulants. And hence it is that we see some patients weeping, others laughing, others sleeping, and others giving vent to their disorder in other forms. It is worthy of notice (a point which has exercised the minds of many men, and is a question disputed as much in the Peripatetic as in the subtle Carthusian school) that this poison has a singular affinity for music, which is said to have a wonderful effect in pacifying and curing those stung by the Tarantula. It has, indeed, been noticed that even old men, and those who are almost overcome by the virulence of the poison, have, as soon as they heard the sound of music, begun immediately to stretch their fingers and their limbs, and then to move the rest of their body so quickly and so accurately to the tune which is played that they seem to surpass young men in their vigour and dancing-masters themselves in their skill. Whether, then, the close connection of this poison with music is to be derived from the peculiar nature of this tuneful creature, we shall consider at greater length below.

§ II. EXAMINATION OF THE NATURE OF THIS POISON IN THE LIGHT OF THE PRINCIPLE OF FERMENTATION.

The character of this poison becomes, I admit, more difficult to define after the explanation I have given, and, I might almost say, is to be placed among those things, the discovery of which is placed as a goal for human invention. Yet if we can make any assertion in matters which are difficult of apprehension, and in which a desire for their discovery is all we can indulge in, it is worthy of notice that the principle of fermentation, which modern thinkers have received in a more enlightened condition, and understood in a stricter sense than before, does seem to throw some light on the clearing up of the nature of this poison. Just as a mad dog does, by its bite and by means of its saliva, that is by the volatile nature of the salt of its body, and the incubation of bad secretions, present an appearance of some fury breeding within it, which is called in medicine hydrophobia, or better, synanche (as D. Meibomius, in one of his elegant treatises cleverly shows in quoting from Josephus Aromatorius); so by its bite the Tarantula inoculates those whom its stings as it were with the evil power of its own virulence, by virtue of an incubation or fermentation which is of a more venomous type. For as the whole idea of the plant lies hidden in the seed of the vegetable, which, on the approach of spring, when the earth is swelling and bursting with her own increase, and the heat of the sun comes and takes part in the forwarding of the process of ripening, is awakened, made to sprout and perfected; so also, in an extremely small particle of what I call "ferment," which is transferred by the sting of the Tarantula into the human body, and immediately afterwards begins gradually to grow, the whole nature of the symptoms is hidden, though they afterwards come out in various forms, according to the character of the patient, his fancy, I believe, being smitten as well as his spirits, by the power of this foreign fermentation. This also happens in the case of bites from other mad animals, the result of which is madness, varying according to the nature of the creature that inflicted the sting. There are some who think that the patient sometimes imitates the animal by which it has been stung. This we learn among others from Felix Plater. Unzerus, treating of this subject in his little work on epilepsy, quotes the following two tragic instances from the book of Heinrich on Monstrosities, cap. 15. The one is that of a girl of Wratislaw, the other of a man, whose name is not given. The man having fed on sow's milk is said to have become greatly enamoured of filth. The girl, who in order to cure the epilepsy with which she was attacked, partook of cat's blood, is said to have assumed the character of that animal, imitating the call, leaping, gesture and walk of the creature. Unzerus does not think this story unlikely because it is to their blood and spirit that the temperament and actions of animals owe their birth. Unzerus is altogether at fault in what he brings forward as an explanation of this. Why, forsooth, if the blood of one animal drunk by another can frequently change its character, why do not wolves, after sucking the blood of sheep, take on the nature of the sheep? and why do not weazels, when sucking the blood of chickens, lay aside their savage nature? The reason is that the nature of these creatures is, as Andrew Libavius elsewhere argues, too "energetic," and changes the food more violently than it is changed by the food. Although they appear to be invited to some show of gentleness, yet seeing they return to their former native ferocity, this stronger movement overcomes the weaker, and the weaker is transformed by the stronger, not the stronger by the weaker. However that may be, the peculiar virtue inherent in the blood for changing the temperament is beyond controversy. Nor is this the case with blood only, but it is true of milk. Nay, the same may even be said of sweat. The quality and power of milk for changing the temperament of children, and the need of caution in selecting nurses, if the mother herself be unequal or too weak for the task, has been fully and acutely commented upon, among others, by Gellius, in his *Attic Nights*. On the subject of sweat and of its ingredients we have a somewhat full account, with notes of experiments from Lepida, to be found in Scaliger.* He gives the following account in his usual brief way:—" The Aracan King," he says, " thus tries the temperament of his wife. He chooses twelve virgins, all of the same age, and orders them to

---

* Exerc. 109. De Subtilitate contra Cardanum.

be completely covered over with woollen cloths. They have then to remain at mid-day diretcly beneath the sun's rays in the highest floor of the house. After they have perspired, which they do profusely under the circumstances, the smell on each set of the garments is tested. Those whose garments smell offensively he gives to his friends for wives, those whose garments smell sweetly he keeps for himself. To prevent deception, the name of the father and mother of the maiden is written on the clothes." So much for that. From this we learn that even in sweat itself there are points worth observing. Nor, again, is it difficult to see that very considerable virtue in changing the character of the blood and spirits resides in the discharged secretion which the Tarantula imparts to the bite at the moment of inflicting the sting. Whether women can also allure men to a love of themselves by means of drugs compounded of their own blood and sweat, I studiously pass by with a brief remark, because I remember I refuted this statement more at length elsewhere. I have stated above that this poison of the Tarantula acts like fermentation. The whole question now comes to this—What is the meaning of this fermentation, which in such small quantity acts more quickly in some and slower in others, but which exercises such great and wonderful power in all?

§ 3. An Account of the Differences between this Tarantula Poison and the St. Vitus's Dance, as well as of certain kinds of Convulsions.

The kind of madness, or as it is called the St. Vitus' Dance (clearly from a superstition that, by the help of St. Vitus, the patients were believed to be restored to a better mind, that is to themselves), seems to have some affinity with the sting of the Tarantula. Those affected with this malady are as delirious and restless as those bitten by the Tarantula, and become so engrossed in dancing and running about that they ultimately become quite exhausted and fall on the ground. In connection with this it is worth while referring to the account given by Tulpius, a famous doctor, of a man wretchedly tormented with the disease, but which it is better to read in the Author's own words than in mine. " This species of madness, which is called by Platerus Felix Vitus's Leap, brings on either endless dancing or restless running about. An instance of this kind of malady it was my lot once to witness near Cortacum, a small town of Flanders, in the case of a very wretched man. The poor creature used to run about for days and nights, with such constant leaps and endless agitation, that his whole body was bathed in perspiration. Yet he did not on this account cease his movements in the very least, but was so entirely given over to this continual movement, that he never gave himself any peace, unless when exhausted nature demanded her dues of sleep." So far for this case. This account is but little different from another given by the great Felix Plater to the same purpose, with the fame of his name and the skill of his profession, to substantiate his statement.* It is about a woman, who danced on the ground for a whole month at Basle, and to whom the Magistrates furnished certain strong men, one being insufficient to carry on the dance with her. From such statements we see the connection, as well as the distinction, between the sting of the Tarantula and the St. Vitus's Dance. That is, those who are bitten by the Tarantula have a desire to dance inordinately, and do begin to leap as soon as a sound of music or an instrument is heard. The victims of the St. Vitus' Dance, however, quite apart from any sting from the Tarantula, or bite from any mad animal, are seized with that peculiar kind of madness, and, without any sounds of music, do tire themselves out by their movements. But neither do the St. Vitus's Dance nor the effects produced by the sting of the Tarantula show any signs of any kind of convulsion, for a convulsion takes place

---

* Prax., Bk. i., cap. 3.

quite apart from the will of the patient, a fact it would be wrong to affirm of either of the other two phenomena. Accordingly, the Arabs are censured by Plater for venturing to deduce the origin of the St. Vitus's Dance from a jerky disposition of the limbs. There are admitted to be certain kinds of convulsions, which seem to imitate very closely the nature both of St. Vitus's Dance, and the results of Tarantula bites, but which really are very distinct, as we learn from a consultation of medical authorities which are easily accessible and familiar. I remember, when I was a boy, that in my native place (Lubeck) I witnessed a most extraordinary case, in a very poor man, who, although perfectly well the day before, began one night to labour under a wretched ailment. The muscles of his whole body, especially of his arms and feet, were so affected that he could not walk without moving wildly alternately an arm, a foot, or both together, thus drawing upon himself the attention of passers-by, who looked on him, some in pity, others in wonder. The account of a woman who was seen in Leyden is somewhat similar. She was so terribly afflicted that when she was compelled to walk, her body moved sometimes on one side, sometimes on another, and with a movement like dancing or leaping. The first sight of her in the temple of the Lutherans made me laugh,

while it increased her frenzy. I was soon, however, lead to pity her, when I learned the full
particulars of her case from my intimate friend,
Fürsenius, the present successful Doctor of
Medicine at Hamburg. Such cases, however,
differ completely and entirely, both from the St.
Vitus's Dance and from the effects of Tarantula
bites, if, that is, we except the general nature of
the symptoms. We see this, when we consider
that in the case of Tarantula bites the patient is
induced to dance by a maddened imagination, and
by his spirits which have been irritated by
poisonous elements. In the case of St. Vitus's
Dance, however, though the mind be perfectly
healthy, yet there is a wonderful agitation of the
limbs, corresponding to a kind of leap, the movement being plainly involuntary.

§ 4. AN EXPLANATION OF THE POWER OF
MUSIC IN CURING TARANTULA BITES.

The cure of the bite of the Tarantula by music
receives illustration from a great number of
writers. Although we ought perhaps here to
place the sweating and drastic methods of cure,
yet these do not detract from the recognised
relationship between the poison of the Tarantula
and music. Thus, those who have been bitten,
as soon as they hear a musical air, begin at once
to leap like strong young men, and give them-

selves up to this exercise for whole months on end. The reason of this desire to dance seems somewhat obscure, as we have already mentioned above. Music rouses the hotter passions and softens men's feelings. Some are charmed or entranced by some sounds, some by others. Hence arose that famous advice of Pythagoras, which the great Bartholinus praises.* Pythagoras, when some young men were conducting themselves in such a riotous way that they seemed madmen, ordered the flute-player, whom they had with them, to play them a solemn tune. The result was they returned at once to a modest comportment, as if they were quite sober. The ancients used various measures to rouse different feelings. The Phrygian measure was employed both for fighting and for mental delectation, the Lydian for sharpening the intellect, the Dorian for exciting feelings of purity, the Æolian for soothing the mind's perturbations. The wonderful affinity between poetry, oratory, and music adds force to what I have said. Their power for influencing the feelings of an audience is known to every one. If the movement of our spirits is too sluggish, (as is the case in sadness) there is nothing strange in the fact that they should be revived by the cheering

---

* Quæst. Nupt. 3, in Nuptiis Schumacheri.

and pleasant modulation of music. But if again they are overstrung, they can be restored to order by a proper harmony. Just as love songs are so rendered and sung, that they become sometimes strong, sometimes gentle, now slow and now fast, sometimes giving the effect of an ascent, sometimes of a descent in the scale, according as the Lydian plaint, the Dorian gravity or the Hippodorian revelry prevails, in the same way a corresponding movement in the pulse is found to take place in case of some who are in love, the pulse being found to be sometimes stronger, and sometimes weaker. It is weaker if the person is under fear or sadness, stronger if hope of obtaining his darling come over his mind, and especially on the mentioning of her name. This change in the pulse is so well known that a good doctor can from the mere pulse, and with the necessary precautions, recognise the fire of love lurking in the patient. The story of Erasistratus is well known in the schools of medicine, who, by feeling his pulse, recognised that Antiochus was vehemently devoured by a passion for Stratonice, a concubine of his father's. When she advanced towards him, he noticed the pulse of the young man become variously affected. He informed the father of the symptoms of the malady, and received 100 talents in reward. In the same successful way did Galen learn from the variations of her pulse at the mention of her lover, that the wife of Menippus was captivated by Pylas, a performer in the circus. Forestus (*Observ.* 30) tells a tragic story of maddened love, in the case of a buxom young girl of 22, of good constitution, who, when seized by love for a certain youth, became so wretchedly tortured by a feeling of suffocation or hypochondria or so called hysteria, conjoined with epileptic fits, that she was considered a mad woman. Forestus, however, such was his natural sagacity and medical skill, began to suspect that the young woman was labouring under the effects of love, and this he did by observing her pulse. His suspicions were realised, for having been informed of the youth whom she loved, (for he could get no answers to the questions he put to her or to her mistress) he mentioned his name in her presence, and asked the by-standers what he did, and where this John of Leida dwelt. The girl began to laugh and talk, and her pulse underwent at the same time a wonderful change. Having hitherto explained the affinity between music and our spirits, we have now to deal with the connection between music and the Tarantula, as well as with the poison ejected by this creature. I observed in the very beginning of this treatise, that those who are stung by the Tarantula are so severely injured as to become immediately restless and afflicted with various kinds of pains. I said that they usually run about, or, like those dead, lie on the ground quite overcome. As soon, however, as they hear a tune, they begin immediately, as if rid of their pain, to leap and dance, not merely in an intelligent way, but so quickly as to out-rival the most robust of youths. As soon, however, as the music stops, they return to the unhappy state produced by the bite, as if they were the victims of some fate. Hence harmony is to them in the place of medicine, for by means of it the spirits, nerves and muscles are made to move. Again when the motion is increased, and the pores all over the body are opened, and the sweat poured out, the unhealty atoms, as they are called, of the disease, are cast out, and the virulence of the malady destroyed, which allows then of the application of antidotes, and sweating mixtures in order to effect a cure. Hence I cannot understand why Cardinus denies that the victims of the Tarantula bite can be cured by music; or, to speak in a more philosophic strain, I am unable to see why he denies that the cure of the malady is due to music. His reason for saying so is, that the nature of music makes it quite unequal to the effecting of such a result. I consider therefore that Cardanus quite deserves the criticism he receives at the hands of Scaliger. "You are right," he says, "in denying that the Tarantula bite can be cured by music, for the poison is quenched by the exertions gone through by the patient and the sweat he exudes, which takes the virus along with it, but you ought to have found an explanation of the fact that though overcome by drowsiness after being bitten, the patient is immediately roused up by hearing music. I have seen patients quite languid and weary, who have been roused to such a pitch of heat at the sound of the lute, that the spectators became weary of watching their dancing. During this movement it is that the pain is quieted, the poison being taken from the heart and diffused in every direction, while the mind is relieved from all sense of illness. When the music stops, the patient does not recover immediately, but only by degrees, and when it is repeated the illness disappears. During this whole time the patient is treated with antidotes." These are the remarks of Scaliger. From them we can learn that from this process of cure we cannot altogether banish the power of music. One objection lies in the difficulty why the spirits, nerves, and muscles require the song or musical instruments to rouse them into activity and dancing. A second difficulty is why music can so suddenly cure pains and other symptoms that the patient, seemingly on the brink of the grave, can, as soon as he hears the music, recover strength to dance and leap. A third difficulty is the explanation why our spirits are so wretchedly affected by the bite of the Tarantula. There appears to be some kind of close connection traceable between the spirits of the Tarantula (so to speak) and our own spirits. I shall deal with each of these points separately. In the first place we have the objection that when all parts of the body are impregnated with poison, there is no proclivity to leap and dance, but whenever a tune is heard, the air arouses our spirits and plays pranks on them. Our nerves and muscles are roused to movement and even to dancing and leaping. The more the movement continues, the greater and more profuse is the expenditure of sweat, and the freer do our spirits become, while the particles of poison make their way from the interior to the exterior surface of our bodies. The fact that on the removal of the music the patient returns gradually to his bad symptoms is due to the fermentation in the poison which increases and developes in its passage through the body. This statement is seen to be true both in the case of those who are intoxicated, and of those who are suffering from a burning fever. Those who are suffering from fever, by a wonderfully deranged fancy, and under the influence of the burning force within them, leave their beds and are worked into a state of high bodily excitement, although before neither hand nor foot could fulfil their proper function, and the patients themselves seemed little distant from the threshold of the grave. Again those who are the victims of intoxication show the strength of their body although the day before they may appear exhausted with fiery breathings which rack their whole being, and seem as if scourged with lashes. This mobility and excessive fervour is frequently the cause why even grave men, when they have drunk too much, by the fiery inhalations which have suddenly been carried to their brain, are compelled to dance and act like clowns, flinging their arms and legs about in all directions, and conducting themselves in a way for which they are heartily sorry on the morrow. The case is similar with those who have been bitten by the Tarantula, who evince such a sudden recovery of strength, that it appears due to some supernatural agency. The reason also is clear why the victims of the Tarantula are so grievously affected by its poison. As to how the sounds which are merely brought to our ears can have such a powerful influence in moving our spirits and our minds, it is a doubtful point.

§ 5. Can Music cure other Diseases besides the Sting of the Tarantula?

Alexander,* among other writers, maintains that music is a cure for other ills besides the Tarantula's sting. He tell us that Theophrastus,

---
* Dier. Genial., bk. ii., cap. 7.

the philosopher, a man of wonderful wisdom, the successor of Aristotle in the Academy, who was well known and esteemed in physical and mathematical science, states, that the strains of pipes or lyres and other wind instruments played in a proper manner can cure the bites of vipers. Esclepiades also, the ancient doctor, states the same fact. His opinion was that those who were troubled with frenzy or mental affections could best be restored and cured by harmony and songs. We are told also that Ismenias the Theban cured several Bœotians, who were labouring under hip-joint disease, by playing on the lute. So great do we perceive is the connection between the nature of man and a harmony of sound. The fact that some hip-joint patients were restored to health by some Phrygian strains (as they are called) can be seen from the words of Theophrastus Eresius, which I quote—" One could make them perfectly whole and free from their trouble by singing to them in the Phrygian strain." There are those who affirm that a sound or tune has different effects on different persons, maintaining that it has provoked some to the pouring out of their own blood, while in other cases it has inspired, as it were, new blood and life. The latter fact we learn from Pliny, the former from Scaliger. Scaliger mentions in his treatise on subtilty, written against Cardanus, that it was a sound which roused the effeminate monsters of Cybele to pour out their own blood, while Pliny, as if in praise of Homer, his authority, reminds us that it was by a song that Ulysses or the sons of Autolicus (whom Delecampus mentions in his notes to Pliny as having been meant by Homer) stopped the flow of blood. Whether these statements are overdrawn or savour somewhat of the magical, I pass over without comment, though I may perhaps some day discuss the question. At present, however, my remarks must be general and brief. If music provides a spell, as it were, against the aforesaid troubles, I think it does so by no other means than by the soothing effect of its notes, whereby the movements of the mind are variously stirred. Hence we see, if the story is true, why those so-called effeminate monsters were induced by hearing a sound to pour out their own blood. For whether urged by heat or fury, they cut into their veins, nerves, muscles, or other parts of their body. This, however, opens to us a wide and unexplored field of investigation. With my small powers, and especially with the small space at my disposal, I dare not venture further than I have done. Later, when my studies are more complete, I may venture to return to this subject. Meanwhile, kind reader, fare thee well.

Praise be to God Everlasting!

END OF VOL. III.

[COLLECTANEA ADAMANTÆA. XV.]

Un=Natural History

OR

MYTHS

OF

ANCIENT SCIENCE;

Being a Collection of Curious Tracts on the
Basilisk, Unicorn, Phœnix, Behemoth or
Leviathan, Dragon, Giant Spider,
Tarantula, Chameleons, Satyrs,
Homines Caudati,
&c.,

NOW FIRST TRANSLATED FROM
THE LATIN,

AND

Edited, with Notes and Illustrations,

BY

EDMUND GOLDSMID, F.R.H.S.,
F.S.A. (Scot.)

IN FOUR VOLUMES.

VOL. IV.

PRIVATELY PRINTED.
EDINBURGH
1886

[Collectanea Adamantæa.]

Myths of Ancient Science.

This Edition is limited to 275 small-paper and 75 large-paper copies.

[COLLECTANEA ADAMANTÆA.—XV]

Un=Natural History
OR
Myths
OF
ANCIENT SCIENCE;
Being a Collection of Curious Tracts on the Basilisk, Unicorn, Phœnix, Behemoth or Leviathan, Dragon, Giant Spider, Tarantula, Chameleons, Satyrs, Homines Caudati,
&c.

NOW FIRST TRANSLATED FROM THE LATIN,

AND

Edited, with Notes and Illustrations,
BY
EDMUND GOLDSMID, F.R.H.S.,
F.S.A. (Scot.)

IN FOUR VOLUMES.

VOL. IV.

PRIVATELY PRINTED.
EDINBURGH.
1886.

On Chameleons,

BY

ISAAC SCHOOCKIUS.

On Chameleons,

BY

ISAAC SCHOOCKIUS.

(1680.)

CHAPTER I.

The Chameleon does not live on air alone. Pliny and Tertullian criticised.

The question of the Chameleon living entirely on air will be our first point of investigation. An affirmative opinion indeed is fully defended by Bustamantinus, a writer of great learning in other respects, and the last likely to give credence to fables. (*On Reptiles*, Bk. v. chap. 15.): a similar position was taken by Pliny long ago (*Nat. Hist.* Bk. vii. chap. 33) where his words are to the following effect: "The Chameleon would be of the shape and size of the lizard were it not that its legs are straight and longer, its movements slower like those of the tortoise ; its body rough like the crocodile ; its eyes placed in hollow sockets, of keen powers of vision and somewhat large and of the same colour as its body. It never opens them or moves the pupils, but keeps gazing with the whole eye. Alone of animals it is sustained without food, drink, but only air." Tertullian agrees thoroughly with this passage of Pliny in his pamphlet on the Pallium, chap. 3. where an African writer is quoted to the following effect : "The creature is a quadruped, is found in the fields, is a gentle and altogether insignificant animal. But he who hears the name chameleon with some previous knowledge of what it means, fears it even more than the lion. It never eats anything, and keeps unimpaired the brightness of its skin ; it feeds with its mouth agape, and ruminates while its sides pulse like bellows. Its food is the air." So much for Tertullian. The words of this passage "It never eats anything and keeps unimpaired the brightness of its skin," have been accepted and illustrated by Salmasius.

If indeed we had extant the work of Democritus, that most industrious student of natural objects, which he wrote, as the learned Plutarch tells us on the subject of the Chameleon, everything would be clear, and free from doubt. Meanwhile, although we are without this treasure-house of learning, we ought to remark that Pliny and Tertullian, nay, all the others who follow them as leaders, and as many as follow again the lead of these latter, (among whom we even find the otherwise most learned doctor Joubert, *Parad.* 2.dec. 1.) go astray from the truth. Dalecampius remarked this after Gesner, when referring to the passage of Pliny we have quoted above, and Scaliger, *Exerc.* 196 sect. 4, agrees with them, when giving his diffuse description of this animal, according to the account of John Landius. Brodæus, the diligent critic, also remarks on Pliny when speaking of this account. (6th Bk. of *Miscellanies*, chap. 21.) But before all other authorities we ought to consult John Faber Lyceus, in his elegant commentary (*Index of animals*, chapter on the Chameleon) where he sets himself to explode this wide-spread fable. The same may be said of Crescentius on "*Growths*," to be found in Paul Zacchias, Bk. iv. *Medical and Legal Questions*, (Lib. 1., Qu. 7., n. 11.) "The error has thence arisen that this creature, which resembles a lizard, can live for several days without taking any additional food during that time. For as Cresentius remarks, "after the creature has swallowed one fly after another (which it passes into its throat with extraordinary rapidity by means of fts forked tongue, on which they are caught by a slimy substance) the process of digesting these takes up several hours, and it subsists on nothing else for several full days, seven or eight in number, I am sure. Hence we see the mistake committed by those who, from the Chameleon, contended that air had the power of nutrition. Such an idea, though receiving the support, not only of Rondeletius, (Bk. i. *on Fishes*, chap. 33) but of the subtle Argentarius, (*Commentaries ii. in prim. Hippoc. Aphoris.*) is yet quite alien from the truth : unless, of course, one intended to mean by the word "aliment" anything that formed an addition or gave a help to a function, as was done by Hippocrates in his book on Diet ; because it cannot be denied that by the inhalation of the air we receive a help in preserving life. *

CHAPTER II.

The Chameleon assumes all sorts of hues except red and white. Reason given for this fact, and passages of several authors illustrated.

Having demolished the opinion of those whom we spoke of in the last chapter on the Chameleon, we have for the present determined on an investigation into the question whether this creature can

---

* Consult Caleb John de Mey " *Sacred Physiology,*" page 150.

assume every kind of colour. The affirmative answer to such a question is maintained by Aristotle when speaking of this animal, (which is placed among the unclean kind of food in Levit. chap. ii. v. 30 and is frequently met with in Syria and Palestine.) From Aristotle, Bk. ii. chap. ii. of "*History of Animals*," Pliny, *Nat. Hist.* Book viii. chap. 33. Solinus, chap. 43 and Elian, Bk. ii. chap. 14, we gather the following statement : the Chameleon does not present only one and the same colour. If, for instance, one meets it of a black colour, it changes and quickly transforms itself into a green ; then, as if by a change of skin, it presents still another appearance, by putting on a white colour, just as an actor puts on a mask. Such being the case, one would say that although it may not rub and smear its body with poisons like a Medea or Circe, it is yet in itself a creature of poison and witchcraft. This gave rise to Plutarch's remarks on the difference between a flatterer and a friend. A flatterer, he says, acts just like a chameleon ; for just as the latter can show us all colours except white, so the flatterer being unable to excel in those things which are worthy of pursuit, imitates everything base as far as he can. So much for Plutarch. The comparison drawn by Casiodorus, (Bk. v. *Various Letters*, Letter 34) between the nature of the Chameleon and the deceiving debtor, is quite as clever. Unwilling to defend himself in court, ignorant of his promise, terrified when caught, he breaks his word, changes the principles he admits, and, not content with one meaning for his words, he puts on various disguises. A Chameleon is very similar in form to the serpent ; it has a golden coloured head, and while the rest of its members are of a whitish tinge, its body is marked by a bright green hue. When one looks at it, and its own speed cannot avail it to escape, in the utmost terror it changes its colours into various others, and appears now blue, now white, now green, now purple. For the same reason Alcibiades received the name of Chameleon, as Plutarch tells us. Again, Socrates (Bk. i., chap. iii. *Hist.*) says ὡς χαμαιλέοντες μετάβαλλον, that is, they changed about like Chameleons. Many indeed, to return to our subject, have determined to accept this as quite fabulous, but if we accept red and white, the Chameleon does take on every colour, as is shewn by John Faber Lyceus quoted in the last chapter, when he cites eye-witnesses on each point. Pliny likewise makes an exception of both of these colours, in the passage quoted. He says: "And the nature of its colour is more wonderful ; for it changes it both on its eyes, its tail, and its whole body with great quickness, always assuming another colour after the former has disappeared."

Nazianzenus, indeed, excludes white like Plutarch. In Oration 3 he says : " The Chameleon is said to easily change colour, and suddenly to assume all hues, with the one exception of white." Although the description by Aristotle of this animal is, as usual with him, very accurate, yet, when speaking of its colour and its changes, he says simply : " When inflated with air it changes its colour." Meanwhile, we evidently cannot think of listening to John Hesronita and Gabriel Sionita, seeing that in the pamphlet which they submitted to the Nubian geographer Arabi, (chap. 9.), they try to make out that all these authors are liars. Nor are the colours which the animal assumes merely apparent, as some have supposed, but real. They are produced, indeed, just as pallor is in man when terrified, or a blush when he is ashamed. For when the blood is received into the inward parts of the body, pallor is the result, as blushing is the result of the blood coming to the surface. Hence also from the character of the sensations, which, in the case of the Chameleon, is manifold and frequently varying, on the humour being excited, the exterior surface of the body changes colour. Now, that which is accustomed to happen to man in the face alone, takes place, in the case of the Chameleon, over the whole body. The reason of its not assuming a red colour is that it has a very moderate supply of blood, which accordingly remains persistently in the neighbourhood of the creature's heart. Again, it does not assume a white colour, because there is in its body no humour to which that colour is natural. Again, as in man, the blood is red and the bile yellow, so likewise the body of the Chameleon contains various humours marked by their own peculiar colours, from the different mingling of which, various colours, corresponding to the various affections of its mind, are produced, which, though coming quickly into, and disappearing quickly from view, yet it cannot be doubted are real. It is indeed from the fact of its assuming such various colours that this creature seems to derive its name. For as Bustamantinus rightly observes (Bk. v., chap. 14, *on Reptiles*), it gets the name χαμαίλεον in Greek, from χάμα, "labour," and λέω, "I see," as if it meant a "laborious or difficult sight," because it is transformed into so many colours that there is difficulty in recognising it as the same. (Read Michael Apostol., Param. p. 260.) The Chameleon is like the lizard, which is said to have a strong love for man, and often to gaze at him for a very long time as if enjoying such a sight, an enjoyment which it seems to express even by its movements, for it frequently moves its tail, and fawns upon him like a dog or other domestic animal. Again, when it sees a serpent lurking in the grass, it is said to use stronger gestures in order to, as it were, warn man by this redoubled movement against the poison by the serpent. Here we have a very striking picture of those who are naturally endowed with the poison of wickedness, and neither seek nor are capable of anything but laying snares for, and attacking others, but who are, by a divine providence, so governed in their conduct, that they are made the unwilling instruments of good to others. There is a remarkable instance of this in the case of Balaam, who came with the intention of cursing but was compelled to bless. There is another in the case of Pharaoh, who, though determined to destroy the Jews root and branch, was forced to send them away and equip them with an immense supply of provisions for their journey. Again, we have the truth enunciated in the Proverbs of Solomon : "When the ways of a man please the Lord, he turns even his enemies towards him." Our enemies frequently become our benefactors by the will of God.

We read that lizards do not breed in England, but of this fact I cannot speak with the certainty of experience. (Consult the Posthumous Zoological Works of Caleb John Sperlingius.) As the Chameleon cannot imitate red or white, so also tyrants can copy every kind of life except that of the upright man. Nazianzenus in his 47th oration brings the charge against Julian of being able to do everything of every kind like the Chameleon or Proteus, but yet of being incapable of feeling compassion towards the Christians. Again, the nature of the courtier is like that of the Chameleon when he copies the black and evil habits of his prince, but cannot represent the pure and chaste traits of his character. Princes give easy access to those clever men who can administer to their sensual desires. A. Marconnet (Bk. ii. Hist.) says that flatterers have destroyed many princes. Batavians call a Sycophant *een craijer*, *een stoevert*. The malediction bestowed on calumniators has become proverbial, as well as on those who raise vexatious law actions. The word Argive means a calumniator : *Die liever een war beesst, dan reet gelt*. For antiquity noticed that the Argives of old were sycophants, and very fond of lawsuits. [Consult And. Canonber on Calumny Delation and Detraction': Also my own dissertation on Delatores in my note on Tacitus, Bk. iv., chap. 30 of the " *Annals.*"]

On Bears licking their Offspring into perfect shape,

BY

ISAAC SCHOOCKIUS.

On Bears licking their Offspring into perfect Shape,

BY

ISAAC SCHOOKIUS.

The falsity of the Statement that She-bears give Birth to a shapeless and bloody Mass instead of a properly developed Fœtus which they perfect by Licking. Origin of the Fable.

Our authorities for the statement that she-bears give birth to a shapeless mass of flesh, which they perfect by licking, are Aristotle (c. 30, Bk. iv *Hist. Animal*); Elian (Bk. ii., chap. 39, and Bk. x., chap. 36.); Oppian (Bk. de. Am. prol.); Ovid in the 15th book of his Metamorphoses writes:

> Nec catulus quem partu reddidit ursa recenti
> Sed male viva caro est, lambendo mater in artus
> Fingit ; et in formam quantam caput ipsa reducit.

Virgil, the prince of poets, is himself said to have declared that he brought forth verses as bears bring forth their young. (Gell. Bk. vi., chap. 10.) It was with this idea in his mind that Bersmanns, the most refined of German poets, wrote and bequeathed us this epigram :

> Ut nullo Musis interpellente vacaret,
>   Parthenopes adiit rura quieta Maro :
> Ursaque lambendo catulos ceu format inertes
>   Cudebat versus sic poliendo suos.
> Assidua docti sua limant carmina cura
>   Et sub judicium singula verba vocant.

Julius Pollux (Onomast, Bk. v., chap. 12,) Philo. (*Hist. Anim.* chap. 12 ;) and lastly, Isodorus ought to be consulted, and it may not be amiss to quote the words of the last named (Bk. 12, chap. 2). They are somewhat to the following effect : " The bear, or ursus, is said to be so called because it orms the fœtus with its mouth or 'os,' as if it were called ' orsus ' instead of ' ursus.' For it is said that these creatures bring forth a shapeless offspring, and that a mass of flesh is born, which the mother forms into the several members by a process of licking. Hence comes the belief that the she-bear after parturition brings the fœtus into shape with her tongue. It is however the immaturity of the birth that causes this, for parturition takes place on the thirtieth day. The result is that a hurried but shapeless birth is produced.

The head of the bear is not strong : its greatest power lies in its legs and shoulders. Hence they sometimes stand upright." So says Isodorus. All such statements, however, are, (with all due deference to so many great men), little in accord with the truth. Hunters undeniably prove that when they have taken pregnant she-bears, and cut open their bodies, they have found the young perfectly formed in all their parts. The faith which Rittershusius (ad. d. l. Oppiani) places in the statement of such hunters, allows me to claim him as of my opinion in regarding this tale of the she-bear in the light of a fable.

The cause of the error is clearly threefold.

I. Certain writers, among whom is R. David Kimchi, (chap. xiii., think that the young of the bear is so encircled in thick folds within the womb that it appears to be embedded therein, and the mother has to diminish this obstruction by the use of her teeth. This opinion is favoured by Cl. D. Joachim Camerarius (Cent. 2. Embl. 21. It must be granted that most quadrupeds bring forth their young wrapped up in folds of skin, and that they not only disengage this covering but even eat it. Any one can prove this by the evidence of his own eyes, in the case of cats and dogs.

II. Others believe that this idea takes its rise, like many others, from the hieroglyphics of the Egyptians, because these people when wishing to picture an uncultured man, but one who is gradually advancing, used to draw the figure of a pregnant bear. (Ho. Apollo, Bk. ii., chap. 8.)

III. The opinion of Julius Cæsar Scaliger has many upholders. He thinks that a circumstance, which takes place in the case of all the brutes, through being observed with special care in the case of the she-bear, has given rise to the fabulous story.

The following are his remarks, (Exerc. 182, Sect. 2.): "It is said that she-bears bring their shapeless fœtus, which present the appearance of formless balls, into shape by their tongue. The falsehood of such a supposition I have shewn elsewhere, for every animal licks its young to make it free from impurities." In all of the above views the presence of truth enables each to be capable of a defence proportionate to that truth. The second of them, however, is far the most probable in our estimation. For, as we shall have very frequent occasion to shew in these books, Egypt was beyond all other countries the most learned in making and fashioning fables, and deceived the poor confiding Greeks in thousands. Cousult Caleb Senguerd, *Physic. Exercitat.* p. 151. A story is told of a bear which carried away a girl to a cave, kissed her every day, chose for her the ripest and fairest of wild apples and pears, and offered her them to eat with all a lover's solicitude.

John Saxo and Olaus Magnus, write that the Danish Kings had a bear for the progenitor of their race, which stole away a very beautiful virgin who bore a son to the vile creature, elegantly shaped, but very hairy, whom she called Ursus, after his father. Nierembergius has shewn that this cannot be literally believed. We cannot think that from the intercourse of a man and a brute a real man can possibly be produced.

The sense of touch is very strongly developed in the snout of the bear. Hence, when struck on that part of its body its anger is great. This is the origin of the saying "Do not meddle with a bear's nose; that is: Do not meddle with those who can work you mischief. Again, we have the phrase "to lead by the nose." He is said to be lead by the nose who can be lead beyond what he knows himself to be right at the dictation of another. The metaphor is taken from animals of the stag order, who are lead about by a ring placed in the end of the snout, just as horses are guided by a bit. The bear delights in the sound of music of which it is passionately fond. Paulus Diaconus and Olaus Magnus tell us that in northern localities, shepherds, when surrounded by bears, are in the habit of at once playing on lutes, in order that the bears may be enchanted with the sounds, and they themselves escape the ferocity of the creatures. There are certain kinds of white bears which are amphibious, and which, as Albertus tells us, are as much at home in the water as on land. Heliogabalus used to place bears and such like animals on a couch where were lying friends of his whom he had made drunk. The peculiar characteristic of the bear is its growl. Hence comes the proverb " He growls like a bear with a sore head." The she-bear shows great affection for her young, places them on her breast, and frequently sits on them like a hen on her chickens, to keep them warm. Bears with young are extremely fierce, especially if they are taken from her. Hence, in Proverbs 17, v. 12, it is said: "Rather meet a bear robbed of her whelps, than a fool in his folly." Again, Hosea, 13, v. 8, : "I shall meet them like a bear robbed of its whelps, &c.,": 2nd Samuel, 17, where the counsellors of David are compared to such bears. Of the changing of men into bears we need say nothing, as such a thing.

"Though the bear is present you cannot see its footmarks." This saying is to be understood as applying to obscure matters. The she-bear brings forth her young in winter, after which she seeks a hiding place, and, defying the keenness and bitterness of the cold, awaits the arrival of spring, and never brings out her young before three months have elapsed. When the creature feels herself pregnant, in dread of her travail, as if it were a disease, she seeks out a cave. She enters her lair, not by walking on her feet, but by throwing herself on her back, and thus hiding her footmarks from the hunters. She then drags herself in on her back, and then lies down in peace.

Besides the authors quoted, more information can be got on the subject of the bear in Aldrovandus, Gesner, Franzius, Schottus, Nylantius and Hextor.

On Satyrs, Mermaids, Men with Tails, etc.,

BY

ISAAC SCHOOCKIUS.

On Satyrs and Mermaids,

BY

ISAAC SCHOOCKIUS.

(1680.)

The question of Satyrs discussed, and an explanation given of what opinion should be held on the subject. References made at the same time to passages in several Authors.

Satyrs, commonly called by the Greeks σάτυροι, derive their name from their lascivious propensities, as we are told by the expounder of Theocritus. Again, the word has been taken by the author of the *Etymologicum Magnum* from the virile member which the ancient Greeks called σάθην, because the Satyrs' continual propensity to lasciviousness (a fact on which all authors agree) and also because they are never satiated in this habit. Hence also in Macrobius (Bk. i., chap. 8,) they are called Sathumni, (others among whom Gesner is one, calling them Sathuni) from Saturn who is called as it were Sathimnus from Sathen. Again the Etymology of the term can be referred to the sathen, according to Natalis Comes (*Mythol.*, Bk. v,, chap. 8.) as is indicated by the fact that statues of Priapus are usually placed in gardens to rouse lustful desires.

According to Rhodiginus (Bk. xix, chap. 25, *Lectures on Antiquity*), as told by his translator, (Bk. iii, chap. 40, *Var. Hist.*), the Satyrs were so called from the gape of the mouth, an opinion also shared in by Phonuntus, to whom a Satyr means a symbol of ectasy, or mental excitement. Hence a small Satyr is called by Cicero a Satyricus (Bk. i, *Divination*), and the Ionians called the Satyrs themselves, φήρεας, or Centaurs. By the word Satyr, however, in the present instance, we do not understand either such Satyrs as are spoken of by the poets, or those figures which are drawn with a devilish buffoonery, or lastly those men who may have chanced to bear the name. We refer to the four-footed satyrs. These creatures are very curiously described by Elian, *Hist. Animal*, Bk. xvi, ch. 21, where we find these words : "The traveller over the neighbouring mountains of India is met at the outset by the appearance of very dense valleys in a district called

Corruda. There, creatures bearing the appearance and shape of Satyrs, and with their whole body covered with hair, and furnished with the tail of a horse, are said to abound. These creatures, when not disturbed by hunters, are accustomed to live in the thickest parts of the forest on leaves and fruits. When, however, they hear the shout of the hunters and the baying of the dogs, they retreat with incredible speed to the tops of the mountains, for they are used to pass over these heights. They easily keep off their pursuers by rolling down huge stones from the top of the mountains, by the force of which many of the hunters are frequenty killed. Accordingly, their capture is a very difficult matter, and even those that are taken are only those who are too weak, or are females with young. The former owe their capture to some disease, the latter to the fact of their being pregnant. Those that fall into the hands of the hunters are taken to the tribe called the Prasii, on the banks of the Ganges." Such are the words of Elian. Pliny, in describing the same animal, wrote as follows : " It is a quadruped, an inhabitant of the tropical mountains of India, and extremely fleet of foot ; it has a human shape, but has the feet of a goat and has the whole of its body covered with hair. It has none of man's habits, but delights in the thickets of woods, and avoids all intercourse with human beings," (Bk vii, chap. 3.) The description of Hieronymus differs somewhat from these remarks of Pliny. (Life of Antonius the Hermit.)

"It was," he says "a human being with hooked nose, and had a forehead on which grew horns, the extremities of its body ended in the feet of a goat." Ptolemy in his *geography*, (Bk. vii., chap. 2.) makes out two islands of the Satyrs, opposite the coast of India and beyond the Ganges, the inhabitants of which are described as having tails like those we find in pictures of the Satyr. These islands Pausanias calls "The Satyrian Islands." When treating of the kingdom of the Greeks, he mentions their existence on the extreme coasts of the sea in the following words :—" When I was carrying on my investigations as to the nature of the Satyr, and which went beyond any previous efforts, I had very frequent opportunities of speaking with persons on the subject. Euphemius Cares told me that on a voyage he made to Italy, he was driven out of his course by the violence of the wind, and carried to the limits of the ocean which were quite out of the ordinary track of navigation. He said there were there islands, many in number, and desert, but inhabited by wild men. At some of these the sailors refused to put in, because certain of them who had been driven on the coast, and experienced the barbarity of the inhabitants, after a voyage of many days had reached the place they were then at. The sailors, he said, called these islands the Satyr islands. They declared the inhabitants of them were red, and had a tail which was not much smaller than that of a horse." These are the words of Pausanias.

Although, however, it has been attempted to ascribe such Satyrs to the class of mankind, yet except some sort of similitude in shape and figure, they have nothing of the human about them. This is noticed by Mela, (Bk. iii., chap. 9.) and Pliny follows him. (Bk. viii., chap. 54.) The latter does not indeed hesitate, (Bk. v., chap 8) to refer the creatures to the class of Ape.

Some have a suspicion that whatever has been said by the ancients on the subject of the animal called the Satyr, is a complete falsehood. But to such we have to oppose the words of a very experienced doctor of Amsterdam, Dr. Nicolas Tulpius, (*Observ. Medic.*, Bk. iii., chap. 56) where his words are to the following effect : "Although it is outside the subject of Medicine, I shall yet annex to this subject a note in evidence of the Satyr of India. Within our own time one was brought from Angola and given as a present to Prince Frederick Henry. This was a fourfooted Satyr, but by the Indians it gets a name derived from the human species, namely Orang-Outang, or man of the woods. It is as long as a boy of

c

three, and as thick as one of six years. Its body was neither fat nor thin, but of a square shape, and it was extremely agile and swift. Its limbs were extremely tough and had huge muscles, capable of doing and daring everything. In front it was quite smooth while behind it was bristly and covered with black hairs. Its face was a distorted copy of that of man, while its nose was flat and hooked like that of a wrinkled and toothless old woman. Its ears indeed were just the same as those of man. The same may be said of its breast which was like a female's; and its stomach had a navel, though somewhat deeper than that of man. Its limbs, both upper and lower, were as like those of man as one egg is like another. Its elbow had the proper joints; its hand the same number of fingers, its thumb the same shape as that of man; it had thighs, and there was an ancle in its foot. The result of this skilful and orderly adaptation of its limbs was that it could walk erect, and it could lift as lightly as it could transfer easily, any very heavy weight which might be given it. When about to drink it grasped the handle of the jug with one hand, and supported the bottom of it with the other, and it wiped away the moisture left on its lips as neatly as the best trained waiter. It displayed the same dexterity when going to lie down. Bending its head upon the coverlet, and covering its body with the bed clothes, it ensconsed itself quite as comfortably as the most pampered dandy. Again, the king of Sambacia told my relative, Samuel Blomartius, that these Satyrs, especially the males, in the island of Borneo, have such daring and such strong muscles, that they charged against armed men more than once, and also against defenceless women and girls. Sometimes they were so fired with the desire of them, that they seized and ravished them over and over again. They are extremely addicted to lust (a circumstance which is common to them and the Satyrs of the ancients). Nay, sometimes they are so wanton and lustful, that the women of India have a greater dread of groves and thickets, than they have of dogs or snakes, for in the former these wanton creatures are always lying hid. The truth of all this leads us to the conclusion that the ideas of ancients were drawn from them." Such are the words of Tulpius. As in the first place it is clear from this passage that Ptolemy (though others have thought differently), was not altogether deceived when he spoke of the "Islands of the Satyrs," so in the second the ancient idea of the great lustfulness of these creatures receives confirmation. The passage of Pausanias, already partly quoted, is here also in point. He tells us there, that Euphemius Cares said to him, that when they arrived at the Satyr islands, the Satyrs, as soon as they saw them, ran down to the ship, and uttered a sound which was no voice, but a kind of horrible and inarticulate shriek. But when women had landed there, they laid hands on them, and attacked them so furiously that they could with difficulty, though beaten with torches, be driven away, and kept from doing them harm. The sailors, fearing they might suffer injury, kept on board the ship, which they anchored at a distance from the shore, but exposed on the shore a barbarian woman whom they had with them. This woman, after most obscene gestures made by the creatures, was the victim of their lust, not only " in cunno, sed etiam in toto corpore." This story of Pausanias recalls the account which Philostratus gives of a heard of Satyrs which were seized with a desire for Olympus. " A herd of Satyrs," he says, " when seized with desire, with flushed and smiling face gazes intently on a young one of their kind, now seeking to touch his breast, now to clasp his neck, and again to snatch a kiss. They all scatter flowers over him, and adore him like a statue. Then the wisest of them snatches a reed which has been warmed by his tongue, and eats it, and by this act he believes he kisses Olympus, and has even a taste of its spirit." Such is the account given by Philostratus. Passages from Lucian and other authors could be quoted in scores in support of this. The remarks of the learned Tulpius have been personally confirmed to me by several sailors in Holland, and others who have traversed the coast of Africa. They say that in various places similar wild beasts are found, and are commonly regarded as coming under the class of apes, of which there are many kinds. Thus it is not necessary to suspect the trustworthiness of the ancients. Many other kinds of prodigies, outside the ordinary kinds of animals, attract the attention and wonder of the learned and vulgar. Ulysses Gesner and other writers state that in the sea and Nile mermen have been seen and captured. They also cite cases of Satyrs, men of the woods, and men completely covered with hair. It is said that a mermaid was captured in a lake in Holland in 1403, A.D., and that she was brought to Haarlem, and lived for many years. She learned to wear her hair over her neck, and perform many other of the tasks of a woman, but she remained perfectly mute to the end. In 1526 a sea-man with beard and hair is said to have been captured in Frisia, who, after living for several years, was at length cut off by a plague. Ulysses Aldrovandus has published a complete book on the subject of monsters, on every page of which many statements worthy of remark occur. "He tells us," says he of Augustine, "that when preaching the gospel in Ethiopia he saw several men and women who

had no heads, but with eyes placed in their
breasts, and with the rest of their members like
our own." Ulysses thinks that these creatures
had really no neck, and that this made their eyes
seem in their breast, because the head was immediately connected with the thorax. Read " Story
of an Indian Satyr brought to Holland," among
the medical observations of the reverend doctor
Nicholas Tulpius. On the subject of sea-men,
many curious and remarkable facts can be found
in P. Nylant and John Hextor.

On People with Tails.

Leaving the subject of the Satyrs, we shall con-
veniently pass on to a discussion as to people with
tails. At first sight it would appear that their
existence was a fact, for Pliny (Bk. vii., chap. 22.,
Hist. Anim.) mentions that in India men are born
with hairy tails; Paul Venetus again in Bk. v.,
chap. 18., of his own Journeys, says that in the
kingdom of Lambrum "men are found who have
short tails like dogs, and they live not in cities,
but in the mountains." In the island of Nemaneg
in the Eastern Sea, there is a nation of tailed men.
In spite, however, of the testimony of Cardanus,
(On Subtilties. Bk. 18.), that a boy who had
been brought up by wild beasts in the island of
Misnia, had not only contracted wild habits, and

had the face and nails of a wild beast, but had even grown a tail: in spite of the evidence of Albertus Magnus (Bk. xxii., chap. 1., *On Animals*, Tract 1.) that two men were born in a wood in Germany who had tails; in spite again of the fact that the great Bartholinus mentions a Danish boy who had a tail—in spite of all this, we maintain it is quite false that men with tails are anywhere found in any quarter of the globe. The story commonly told about the early English receiving tails through the curse of Augustine, the Apostle of Gregory the Great, must be considered a complete falsehood: and they are quite in the dark, who believe that this people has the *os coccygis* either higher up or longer than is usual. This idea seems to have arisen from the fact that some men in Dorsetshire, intending to insult Augustine and his companions, fastened the tails of ray fish to their clothes, as Genebrardus, quoting from William of Newburg's Chronicles, tells us. The above statements appear more probable than those which John Major mentions (*De Gestis Scotorum*, Bk. ii., chap. 9.) where the following account occurs:—" Augustine on crossing over to Dorsetshire on a mission to England, organised by St. Gregory the Great, began to preach the Gospel. But the common people in ridicule held forth the tails of fishes to the man of God. Therefore, Augustine prayed to God on his knees, that for the punishment of this sin, the children of the district should be born with tails, and that by this warning they should learn not to despise God. And by reason of this, as the annals of England tell us, children were born with tails. It is not at all then from the influence of the climate that they had tails. Nor do I think that, at the present time, men are here born with tails, but the tribe was afflicted with this punishment until such time as they might feel trust in God's servant. I give no assent to those Scotchmen and Frenchmen who maintain the opposite view. There is also said to be a tribe of this nature in Spain." In the case of a Danish boy indeed, as Bartholinus in the passage above cited tells us, there seemed to be a tail formed from the large number of bones and cartilaginous formations in the *os coccygis*. Weinrich describes various monsters, and speaks of a boy born at Cracow in Poland, in 1594, from whose back there hung a live serpent, which still kept gnawing at his dead body. This however, can be accounted for by some disease under which the pregnant mother was labouring. For if any portion of the *embryo* becoming putrid, gives birth to a sepent, this creature when released, can cling to the remaining part which still remains undecomposed. Thus Pliny (*Nat. Hist.* Bk. ix., chap. 69.) asserts that in Egypt, when the Nile is getting lower, (a fixed annual occurrence), small mice are caught which are partly composed of earth.

Here, and in this regard, I ought to treat of and explain three curious sayings.

I. "One should pull the hairs out of a horse's tail, one by one." For what is impossible to be done by force and violence, can be effected by time and diligence. This is the meaning of the proverb. In German we express the same idea by saying that hens hatch their chickens only by degrees.

II. "You are tying a dolphin by its tail." "You have a hold of an eel by its tail." A apt remark is here made to describe those who have to deal with men of slippery character and doubt ful faith.

III. "A fox is known by his tail." This phrase we are accustomed to use in describing those whose true character comes out when danger appears. The foxes tail is too large for its body, and is so bushy that it cannot easily hide it.

The White Lilies of Palestine.

Our blessed Saviour, in the sermon which he delivered, and which is found in Matthew, chap. VI., v. 28, in order to teach his disciples to be content with their present circumstances, and withdraw them from anxiety about worldly things, uses the following words. "And why take ye thought for raiment? Consider the lilies of the field, how they grow. They toil not, neither do they spin: and yet I say unto you, that even Solomon, in all his glory, was not arrayed like one of these." A parallel passage occurs in Luke. I once heard certain learned men, but labouring under the great tulip mania, who believed that the lilies spoken of by our Saviour, in the above words, were the same as their own tulips, although these men themselves were well deserving of being called 'tulips,' that is, stupid and dull, for in the old Belgic tongue a *tulpe* or *tulpisch* is another word for a silly man. I am quite aware, indeed, that any beautiful flower may be called a lily. It is quite well known that the Sacred Writings do not disagree with such a manner of expression (for in the Song of Solomon, chap. ii., v. 16, the passage occurs, "My beloved feedeth among the lilies," and again, chap. iv., v. 15, "Thy two breasts are like two young roes that are twins, which feed among the lilies.") In the same way we are aware that the Greek word $\lambda\epsilon\iota\rho\iota o\nu$ means any beautiful flower, as has been noted by Hesychius and Suidas, in their remarks on Theocritus, Idyl 19. Again, Homer has more than once the expression, "lily-tinted mouth," and Apollo is, by the same poet, called a lily. Again, Susa, a famous city, is called in Hebrew by a name which signifies a lily. Thus Athenæus (Bk. 12), Eustathius (in Dionys.), and Hesychius called that ointment Sousinum, the principle ingredient of which was taken from lilies. It is also well known that the Narcissus was called lily, for this has been noticed by Theophrastus (*Hist. Plant.* Bk. vi, chap. 6.) I cannot, however, be persuaded to understand that anything else was meant in the words of Christ but the white lily, properly so called, for this alone can compete with the splendour of a Solomon. At first sight this assumption of beautiful workmanship in the lily does not appear justifiable. But let any one take one of the new kind of optical instruments which magnifies minute objects placed near the eye, and look through it at the graceful stamens of this flower, or at its filaments and tissues, and he will be forced to confess that such beauty and wonderful structure surpass the powers of any tongue to express. Pliny has described the wondrous beauty of the structure of this lily (Bk. 21, chap. 6.) I cannot refrain from quoting a few of his words. "The lily," he says, "is next the rose in the scale of beauty, and when placed amongst a bunch of the latter flowers, a very becoming effect is the result. The leaves are much prized in the making of ointment and oil." Such are the words of Pliny. The sun flower of Peru is much taller than the lily, and hence merits the name of giant flower, but at the time of Pliny it was not known. Hence we can see how apt was the name given to this flower by the Corinthians, who called it ambrosia, as Athenaeus tells us. (Bk. xv.) The poets feigned it sprang from the milk which fell on the earth from the sleeping Juno, when Hercules wished to carry her off. Compare Cælius (*Rhòdig.* Bk. vi., chap. 2.) To return, however to the words of our Saviour. From the well known fact that he was accustomed to draw similes from the circumstances of ordinary daily experience, we can understand the great aptness of his introducing the subject of lilies, because even in the present day they grow in great profusion in the valleys of Palestine, as Joh. Cotovicus Ultrajectinus, a knight of Jerusalem, in his description of the Holy Land, following Adrichonus of Delphi, observes. The beauty of the lily is preferred to that of the magnificent dress of Solomon, because the former is natural, while the latter is imitative. Solon also recognised this fact, as we are told by Diogenes Laërtius, (Bk. i.), for being asked by Crœsus, who was blazing in the most spendid ornaments, if he had ever seen a more beautiful sight, he replied that cocks, pheasants, and peacocks, were far more splendidly adorned, for they were clad in natural brightness and surpassing beauty. The lily blossoms, as Anatolius tells us, will remain green for a whole year if, when they are closed after their time of being open for the day is past, they are plucked and placed in earthernware vessels without enamel and paint, and covered carefully up to be put bye. By this means they can be preserved fresh for a whole year. When after a time, they are brought out for use, they instantly expand on being brought into the sun, and feeling its heat. The bulbs, if the flowers are required in succession, or at certain times, are so planted as to be placed some at the depth of two, some of four, and some of eight inches. The lilies will come up on different days by this method, which is also said to be successful with other flowers. An oil is extracted from the flower by bruising, which possesses the power of softening the skin. Some use the bulb to cure sores. (See Ætius, Bk. i., chap., 238.) The rose can be made green, yellow, or purple, by cutting the stem near the roots, or by boring a hole in the tree, and filling the hole or aperture thus exposed with, say, copper rust, if a green coloured rose is wanted; with Indian stone or lapis lazuli well pounded down, if a blue colour is wanted; with saffron, if a yellow effect is desired ; and so on. Lastly, the incision must be tied up and properly plastered over, and protected against external injuries. (Read Joachim Sruppius on *Gardening*.) The rose is a cold and dry plant, and is composed of bitter and astringent substances. Its smell is good for a fever or headache, but bad for a cold, and induces drowsiness. Taken for fevers arising from bile, it has good effects and strengthens the stomach and liver. It affects the the testicles in a peculiar way, and prevent, strong exhalations from being carried to the head. (See Simeon Sethum on *Foods*.) I must now stop as my paper is finished. Meanwhile farewell; and give me your good wishes for my future success!

To God be Thanks and Glory!

THE END.

www.ingramcontent.com/pod-product-compliance
Lightning Source LLC
Chambersburg PA
CBHW031251250426
43672CB00029BA/2088